MATTHEW HENSON

The **African-American Biographies** Series

—African-American Biographies—

MATTHEW HENSON

Co-Discoverer of the North Pole

Series Consultant:
Dr. Russell L. Adams, Chairman
Department of Afro-American Studies, Howard University

Laura Baskes Litwin

Enslow Publishers, Inc.

40 Industrial Road   PO Box 38
Box 398   Aldershot
Berkeley Heights, NJ 07922 Hants GU12 6BP
USA   UK

http://www.enslow.com

Library of Congress Cataloging-in-Publication Data

Litwin, Laura Baskes.
    Matthew Henson : co-discoverer of the North Pole / Laura Baskes
Litwin.
       p. cm.— (African-American biographies)
    Includes bibliographical references (p.   ) and index.
    ISBN 0-7660-1546-7
    1. Henson, Matthew, 1866-1955—Juvenile literature. 2. Afro-American
explorers—Biography—Juvenile literature. 3. North Pole—Discovery and
exploration—Juvenile literature. [1. Henson, Matthew Alexander,
1866–1955. 2. Explorers. 3. Afro-Americans—Biography. 4. North Pole—
Discovery and exploration.] I. Title. II. Series.
    G635.H4 L58   2001
    919.8—dc21

                                              00-009785

Printed in the United States of America

10 9 8 7 6 5 4 3 2 1

To Our Readers: All Internet Addresses in this book were active and appropriate
when we went to press. Any comments or suggestions can be sent by e-mail to
Comments@enslow.com or to the address on the back cover.

Illustration Credits: Courtesy of the Department of Library Services,
American Museum of Natural History, p. 56 (ANMH Neg. 329141), p. 95
(ANMH Neg. 272317); Courtesy of the Peary-MacMillan Arctic Museum,
Bowdoin College, pp. 42, 78; Dartmouth College Library, pp. 37, 107;
Department of Rare Books and Special Collections, University of
Michigan Library, p. 24; Kalman Rusinow Collection, p. 18; Library of
Congress, p. 16; Stamp Design ©1986 U.S. Postal Service. Reproduced
with permission. All rights reserved, p. 113.
    The following photos are © The Verne Robinson Collection of restored photos:
p. 104; composite, p. 97; Library of Congress, pp. 8, 111; National
Archives, pp. 25, 51, 64, 75, 88; Bradley Robinson, *Dark Companion,*
1947, pp. 91, 109; Harper's, February 1907, p. 101; Matthew Henson, *A
Negro Explorer at the North Pole,* 1912, p. 12; Robert Peary, *Northward Over
the "Great Ice,"* 1898, pp. 21, 34; Robert Peary, *Secrets of Polar Travel,* 1917,
p. 46; Robert Peary, *The North Pole,* 1910, pp. 10, 39, 44, 53, 66, 69, 81;
The Outlook, September 18, 1909, p. 30.

Cover Illustration: © The Verne Robinson Collection (Hassan cigarette
card, c. 1910)

CONTENTS

ACKNOWLEDGMENT

The author wishes to thank
Verne Robinson
for his contributions
to this book
and to the legacy
of Matthew Henson.

1

CLOSE CALL

Matthew Henson was headed north once again. It was the summer of 1905 and this was his fifth journey to the Arctic as a member of Commander Robert Peary's world-famous polar exploration team. The group was sailing from New York City on the *Roosevelt*, a newly built steamship that had been designed specially to move through crushing Arctic ice.[1] After fifteen years in the Far North, Henson knew that a vessel as tough as a battleship was going to be needed.

Henson's experience had taught him also that those who hoped to survive in the Arctic needed to be

Once again, Matt Henson was ready to take on the challenges of the Arctic.

as tough as soldiers. This vast, frozen region has temperatures of sixty degrees below zero, months of darkness, and snowy winds that wipe out all visibility for days at a time. So far, the Arctic had defeated all who had tried to conquer it.

But Matthew Henson was a determined competitor. He was convinced that this voyage would be the one. His team would finally grab the prize that had evaded them for so long—to be the first men to reach the North Pole.[2]

After three rough weeks of plowing through the dangerous icy waters, the ship dropped anchor at Ellesmere Island in northernmost Canada. For the first time, the team had reached the shores of the polar ice cap. They could now establish a base camp with the supplies they had brought from Greenland. The North Pole was less than five hundred miles to the north. With winter's end, the men could push forward on foot and by dog sledge.

Commander Peary had a new strategy this time for the assault on the Pole. The expedition would break into two teams: A lead team would travel lightly and forge the trail. Then a main team would follow a few days behind with the bulk of the supplies. The main team would divide into smaller parties that would act as relay teams bringing supplies to the lead team when needed.[3]

Henson was to direct the lead team. He was the

expedition's best dog-team driver and the only one able to speak the native Inuit language. Henson had first come to the Arctic with Robert Peary in 1891 and had accompanied him on every voyage since. Peary's selection of Henson to head up the lead team was a natural choice.

On the last night of February, in an eerie evening twilight, Henson led three sleds onto the sea ice. Almost from the start, he knew they were in serious trouble. An ominous groaning sound could be heard beneath their feet. Warmer than usual temperatures had made the ocean beneath the ice especially rough.

On a trek, the explorers mostly had to push their overloaded sledges in a single line, clearing a trail across the ice.

Pressure from the moving currents was forcing the ice to break up. What seemed to be solid ground would suddenly split open and become water so cold it could kill a person in minutes.

The crew was forced again and again to rush ahead to keep from falling in, or to come abruptly to a halt and wait hours for the temperature to drop and the water to refreeze.[4] After twenty-five days at this nerve-rackingly slow pace, Henson's team was stopped altogether by deep water a half mile across. They had no choice but to set up camp and wait for a freeze that took a week to arrive.[5]

A fierce snowstorm hit two days later. The ice rolled violently underfoot, making many of the dogs seasick. When the blizzard finally let up after six days, the men found that they had drifted seventy miles to the east.[6] The relay teams sending supplies up from base camp now would not be able to find them. If they were to continue, it would be without the promise of food.

Henson and Peary decided to push ahead anyway. They extended their daily marches, allowing themselves only a few hours for rest. Dogs began dying, weakened by the lack of food and the longer run time. The men grew hungrier each day with nothing to eat but frozen pemmican, a mixture of sun-dried fatty meat and fruit.

On April 21, they took a sun observation that showed them to be at 87 degrees 6 minutes north

Despite the extreme hardships he would face, Henson was determined to reach the North Pole.

latitude. This was the farthest north ever recorded.[7] The expedition was within two hundred miles of the North Pole. Yet, after fifty-two days of marching, the men knew that once again the game was up. They had dangerously little food left and they still had to make the long hike back to base camp.

Matthew Henson led the group back. The return trip was an extreme test of his endurance. His weight had dropped from 150 pounds to a skeletal 100 pounds. His eyes ached from the constant glare of the sun, and his chapped skin burned.[8]

Once again Matthew Henson and Robert Peary had been defeated by the severe Arctic conditions. Henson was now forty years old. He had spent fifteen brutal years in this quest with Peary. How much longer could he persevere?

Despite the enormous risks and hardships, Henson knew he would never quit before he reached the North Pole. Somehow he would complete the long and courageous journey that had begun when he was still a boy.

2

SEAWORTHY

atthew Alexander Henson was born on August 8, 1866, in rural Charles County, Maryland, some forty miles south of Washington, D.C. He was the second child of Lemuel Henson and his second wife, Caroline. The Hensons farmed a small plot on the fertile tidewater shores of the Potomac River. They were sharecroppers, meaning that they did not own their land but worked it for someone else and were paid for their labor. For years the family lived peacefully alongside their neighbors. Then, a year after Matthew's birth, their simple quiet life was interrupted forever.

The end of slavery and the Civil War in 1865 had not pleased everyone in the tobacco-growing countryside of southwestern Maryland. Though Maryland chose not to secede from the Union, many slaveowners in this border state sided with the South.[1] Matthew Henson's parents were never slaves, but their color made them a constant target of violent white supremacists.[2]

Caroline Henson died when Matt was a very young child, and years later Matt could not even remember his mother.[3] His father remarried, and with Nellie, his third wife, had more children. (In those days, there were no birth certificates for African-American children born in rural areas, so there are no reliable records naming all of Matt's brothers and sisters.) Nellie, who became Matt's stepmother, was mean-spirited and abusive. Matt was beaten frequently and kept home from school to work the farm. When Matt was eight, his father died in a farming accident. Three years later, Matt ran away from home in the middle of the night. The eleven-year-old made his way to Washington, D.C., and found a job as a dishwasher in a small restaurant owned by an African-American woman, Janey Moore, known affectionately to all as Aunt Janey.[4]

Matt lived with Janey Moore for almost a year. She fed him the same meals she made for the cafe customers and allowed him to sleep on a cot in a corner of her kitchen. For the first time that he could

Matt had a tough childhood, and when he was eleven years old he ran away to Washington, D.C., above. Janey Moore took him in and gave him a job.

remember, Matt was treated well. Yet he also longed for new experiences. When an old sailor and former slave nicknamed Baltimore Jack began telling him exciting tales of life at sea, Matt decided it was time to move on.[5]

Matt knew that the great ships the old sailor spoke of were moored at the wharves in Baltimore. What he did not know when he set out walking to Baltimore was that it was forty miles away. Though it was a long hike, the city did not disappoint him. For a boy with a dream of adventure at sea, the docks of Baltimore were a marvel.

At that time, many three-masted vessels carrying cargo bound for Europe and the Far East began their journeys in the waters of the Chesapeake Bay. Towering and majestic, these ships provided their sailors with hardy employment. Immediately upon his arrival at the port, Matt began looking for a job.

It did not take him long to find one. A ship called the *Katie Hines* was in need of a cabin boy. Captain Childs, whose ship it was, hired Matt on the spot.[6] The *Katie Hines* was due to leave port the next day for a six-month voyage to Hong Kong.

A cabin boy was expected to mop the decks, assist in the galley kitchen, and keep the captain's quarters clean. Matt was diligent at his job from the start, and Captain Childs took notice. This kindly bear-sized man, white-haired and bearded, recognized in Matt a young person with great energy and intelligence.

Captain Childs gave Matt informal lessons in his cabin. The captain taught Matt geography, mathematics, and navigation. They read books on history and literature. The captain shared his love of learning along with his texts, and Matt received an education that went far beyond what he had learned in his short time at school.[7]

During his time on the *Katie Hines*, Matt gained a lot of practical experience as well. He became, he said later, "an able-bodied seaman."[8] Matt learned carpentry by building bunk beds and sea chests and restoring broken beams. He learned to rig the intricate network of ropes and chains that worked the sails and supported the masts. He learned to navigate by the stars.

Matt saw a lot of the world too. At various times, the ship sailed to the Caribbean, Spain, France, Russia, North Africa, Japan, China, and the Philippines.[9] Matt

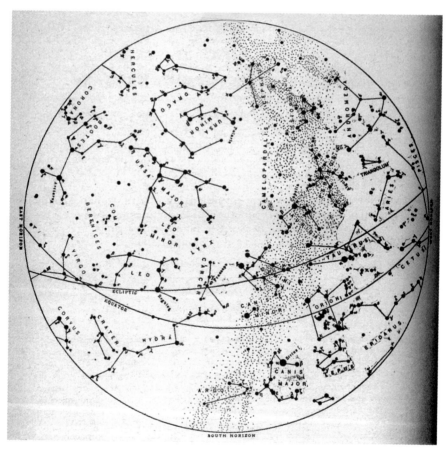

Matt learned to navigate by the stars when he worked as a cabin boy on the *Katie Hines*. The kindly ship captain also taught him geography, carpentry, and many seafaring skills.

sailed with the *Katie Hines* for five years. Then, when Matt was seventeen, Captain Childs became sick with a terrible fever, probably malaria. Matt stayed at the bedside of the dying captain until he was buried at sea off the coast of Jamaica.

Captain Childs had influenced Matt more than anyone else in his young life. He could not imagine staying with the *Katie Hines* after the captain's death. Returning with the crew to Baltimore, he immediately quit his post.[10] But he had no idea just how difficult it would be to find work as challenging as his duties on the *Katie Hines*.

Matt signed on with another ship, the *White Seal*, which was sailing to Newfoundland to hunt seal. The boat was so dirty, and its crew so drunken and irresponsible, that Matt quit as soon as they reached port in St. John's, Newfoundland. He paid his own way back on another ship to Boston.

For the next three years, Matt held various short-lived jobs, none of them at sea. The closest he got to a ship was in Boston, where he worked as a stevedore, a person who unloads a ship's cargo. He worked as a bellhop and a messenger in Providence, Rhode Island. He was a night watchman for a time in Buffalo, New York. He drove a horse and carriage for a wealthy man in New York City.[11]

Matt Henson's opportunities for meaningful work were limited because he was black. The years following the end of the Civil War were especially difficult ones for African Americans. The 13th Amendment to the Constitution had granted liberty to slaves, but there were still many people who did not accept black freedom.

Henson had faced racial bigotry from crewmen on the *White Seal*. This was not the first time he had dealt with prejudice. A sailor on the *Katie Hines* once beat him up and hurled racial slurs. But Captain Childs did not tolerate the ill-treatment of any of his men, and the incident was never repeated.

Sailing with the *Katie Hines*, Henson had been somewhat protected from the kind of prejudice that was common in the United States during the second half of the nineteenth century. Captain Childs was a fair-minded man who considered skin color irrelevant. He expected each crew member to do his job and treat the others with respect. The *Katie Hines* was never in port in the United States for very long. Had Henson spent more time on American shores, he probably would have been confronted earlier with the obstacle of prejudice.

Henson ended up going back to the city he knew best, Washington, D.C. He stayed with his younger sister Eliza and took a job in a shop that sold furs and hats on Pennsylvania Avenue, not far from the White House. It was in 1887 at this store, B. H. Steinmetz & Sons, that a chance encounter changed the course of Henson's life.[12]

As a young man, Henson found that his job opportunities were limited because of his skin color.

A tall thin man with a bushy mustache was shopping for a pith helmet, a hat that provided protection from jungle sun and insects. This man, a navy lieutenant from Philadelphia, had been asked by the U.S. government to go to Nicaragua to find a route for a canal that could link the Atlantic Ocean with the Pacific.

The lieutenant selected a hat. Then he asked the store's owner, Sam Steinmetz, if he knew of someone who might be interested in going on the Nicaragua expedition as his valet.[13]

Steinmetz recommended Matt Henson, and Henson accepted the stranger's offer on the spot. Henson later described his first impression of the lieutenant: "I recognized in him the qualities that made me willing to engage myself in his service.[14]

The naval officer introduced himself as Robert Peary. From that moment on, the names and fates of Matthew Henson and Robert Peary would be forever linked.

3

BLUEPRINT FOR A CANAL

Robert Peary had been to Nicaragua once before he met Matt Henson. Peary had gone there for three months in 1884 on a surveying trip. A surveyor takes careful measurements of an area and draws an exact map of it. For his second trip, in 1887, Peary planned to survey treacherous terrain in the jungle.

The U.S. government was eager to find a place to dig a canal. At that time, all business and travel over water was done by ship. Voyages were long and expensive because to go from the Atlantic Ocean to the Pacific, a ship was forced to sail south all the way

In Nicaragua, Henson helped Robert Peary survey a route for a canal that could link the Atlantic and Pacific oceans.

around Cape Horn at the tip of South America. Ships traveling from the East Coast to the West Coast of the United States had to take this long, out-of-the-way route. A canal connecting the Atlantic and Pacific oceans would change everything.

Nicaragua seemed a logical place to build a canal because it was centrally located on the isthmus (narrow body of land) that is Central America. A company from

France had been trying to find a route in Panama, the southernmost country in Central America, but had not had much luck. (Panama was where the canal ultimately would be built by the U.S. Navy from 1904 to 1914.)

Henson sailed with Lieutenant Peary to Nicaragua on a ship called the *Hondo*. Henson's responsibilities at the outset of the trip were to keep order at the base camp, which mostly entailed doing laundry and carpentry.

With Henson and Peary were forty-five engineers from the United States and one hundred laborers who joined the ship after a stop in Jamaica.[1] The laborers were hired to hack through the dense jungle brush

Matt Henson

Henson, third from left, with the Nicaragua Canal survey team.

with machetes. The engineers needed a clear view to do their survey. The swampy land that was proposed for the canal route was infested with malaria-carrying mosquitoes and poisonous snakes. The tropical heat was oppressive with humidity and almost constant rain.[2]

Peary soon recognized that Henson's skills and strength could be of value in his mission. After four months in the steamy jungle, he promoted Henson to the position of chain man on the surveying team.[3] The surveyors made their measurements with the aid of chains attached to the tops of poles, which served to create straight lines. As chain man, Henson's job was strenuous, requiring a perfectly still hand on the heavy pole. Even the slightest shake on the chain could cause a miscalculation.

In early 1888, after seven months, the survey was finished and the *Hondo* returned home. In Nicaragua, Henson showed that he was able to assist Peary in ways that went far beyond washing clothes. He demonstrated physical strength living in difficult circumstances and was skilled as a carpenter and mechanic. Peary praised Henson's "intelligence, faithfulness, and better than average pluck and endurance."[4] In Washington, D.C., Henson went back to his store clerk's job. The routine of stocking hats and fur coats contrasted sharply with the adventure of the canal survey.

Peary returned to Philadelphia and his job with the

navy. But his mind was not on his work. He was already thinking of taking another trip. In fact, for some months, he had been considering a return journey to an area as different from the tropics of Central America as any place could be.

Almost exactly ten years older than Matt Henson, Robert Edwin Peary had grown up in Maine, where he studied civil engineering at Bowdoin College. After graduation he passed a rigorous entrance examination for the Civil Engineer Corps of the U.S. Navy and was made a lieutenant. His job was to draw plans for and inspect structures, like bridges and piers, that belonged to the navy.

Since the time he was a young boy, Robert Peary had been fascinated by Arctic exploration. He had read every book he could find on the subject and dreamed of adding his name to the long and illustrious list of explorers who had ventured north. Peary sought adventure and fame. At age twenty-four he wrote his mother:

> I don't want to live and die without accomplishing anything or without being known beyond a narrow circle of friends. I would like to acquire a name which would be an "open sesame" to circles of culture and refinement anywhere.[5]

In 1885, Peary took a six-month leave from the navy and booked passage on a whaling ship bound for Greenland. Nothing he had read prepared him for his first visit to the Arctic. In his travel journal he described Greenland as

> an Arctic Sahara, in comparison with which the African Sahara is insignificant. For on this frozen Sahara of inner Greenland occurs no form of life, animal or vegetable; no fragment of rock, no grain of sand is visible. The traveler across its frozen wastes sees but three things in the world, namely, the infinite expanse of the frozen plain, the infinite dome of the cold blue sky, and the cold white sun—nothing but these.[6]

Peary spent three months in Greenland before coming home. Despite the fact that he had not gone very far, the trip whetted his appetite for further exploration—and fame. Now he wrote to his mother: "My last trip has brought my name before the world; my next will give me a standing in the world. . . . Remember Mother, I *must* have fame. . . ."[7]

Peary had two main objectives for a return trip to Greenland. He wanted to be the first person to make a crossing of the huge ice cap and he wanted to discover whether Greenland was an island. Maps at that time left blank the northern extremes of Greenland. Some people believed that Greenland extended all the way to the North Pole.

While Robert Peary made his plans, the Norwegian explorer Fridtjof Nansen, a champion skier, crossed Greenland on skis specially designed for the ice. Peary was crushed when he heard the news. It was reported that he looked "as if he had just seen someone die."[8]

He decided to change his strategy. He reasoned that although he could no longer be the first to cross the ice cap, he might still be the first to explore the unknown northeast section of Greenland. This exploration might even lead to the greatest prize of all—the discovery of the North Pole.

Peary knew that he needed to act quickly. Nansen was not his only competition. Most of Africa had been explored in the preceding decades, and the Arctic and Antarctic remained the last great uncharted land masses. Whoever was first to the poles was likely to become as famous as Christopher Columbus.

Exploring was expensive, and raising the money needed to hire a ship and equipment was not easy. Peary approached a number of wealthy people he hoped would back him, but the awful circumstances surrounding the Greely expedition to Greenland just five years earlier made his job more difficult. (Most of the group led by U.S. Army Lieutenant Adolphus Greely had died. It was rumored that those who lived had resorted to cannibalism.)

Finally Peary was successful in winning financial support for his voyage. He then began the task of assembling a team to go with him. Peary wrote to Matt Henson and asked him to move to Philadelphia. He arranged a messenger's job for Henson with the League Island Navy Yard.[9] Peary expected Henson to

□□□□□□□□□□□□□□□□□□□□□□□□□□□□□□□□□□□□□□

From the time he was a child, Robert Peary, above, was fascinated by Arctic exploration.

use his free hours to help with final preparations for the trip.

Matt Henson had been waiting for word from Peary. In the meantime, he pursued love. After a whirlwind courtship, Henson had just married a vivacious young woman named Eva Flint.[10] He was eager now for his career to begin anew as well. In their first meeting about the voyage, Peary was straightforward: The work he expected of his crew would be extremely physically demanding and he could pay Henson only $50 a year. Even in 1891 this was a very small sum. But Henson saw before him an unusual opportunity for adventure and fame, and he decided that would be compensation enough.[11]

The other members of the team included Frederick Cook, a doctor; Eivind Astrup, an expert cross-country skier from Norway; Langdon Gibson, an authority on birds; and mineralogist John Verhoeff, who agreed to pay $2,000 toward the cost of the trip in return for being allowed to join it. Verhoeff had written to Peary that he "would like to accompany you fully realizing that the chances may be nine out of ten that I would never return."[12]

The last person joining the group was Peary's wife, Josephine, who was not welcomed by the others. John Verhoeff was said to have offered another $500 to Peary if he would send Josephine home.[13] Newspaper accounts lambasted Peary for risking his wife's safety.[14]

Yet "Jo" and "Bert," as they called each other, were determined to make the trip together.

On June 6, 1891, the expedition set sail from a dock alongside the Brooklyn Bridge. Matt Henson would later write that "the impressions formed on my first visit to the Land of Ice and Snow were the most lasting."[15] Yet on that spring day, Henson could not yet know all that lay ahead. The adventure north was just beginning.

4

TRAILBLAZERS

ust before the ship left port, Matt Henson had made a wager that he fully intended to win. An officer at the League Island Navy Yard had bet Henson $100 that he would lose fingers and toes to frostbite in the Arctic. The navy officer believed that Henson's African ancestry made him less able to tolerate a cold climate.[1] Henson knew that this man's view was shared by others and he meant to prove them wrong.

The men were sailing on the *Kite*, a ship that had made many voyages to northern seas to hunt whales and seals. A *New York Times* reporter described the ship as "a dirty and greasy little whaling steamer."[2] Its captain, Richard Pike, was an experienced sailor from Newfoundland. It was Captain Pike who had brought Adolphus Greely to Greenland on his disastrous mission.[3]

Three and a half weeks after leaving the United States, the expedition reached the shores of Greenland. The crew's first impression of the coastal landscape was a gentle one; wildflowers and mosses covered the cliffs above.[4] It was only after climbing to the top of the cliffs that they could view the imposing

The 1891 North Greenland Expedition. Seated, from left: Frederick Cook, Matthew Henson, John Verhoeff, Eivind Astrup, Langdon Gibson. Standing: Josephine Peary, Robert Peary.

ice cap in the distance. It was truly massive: 1,500 miles long and 450 miles wide. And it rose up sharply to plateau at an altitude above three thousand feet.[5]

The *Kite* sailed northward. The lush scenery of Greenland's southern shore was soon replaced by a bleaker, rocky terrain. The sea became icier, and giant floating chunks called floes kept blocking the ship. The *Kite* carefully made its way up the coastline.

Approaching McCormick Bay in northern Greenland, the expedition met with its first accident. Veering away from a floe, the ship's rudder got stuck in packed ice. The rudder is the wooden board that projects below the ship and helps to steer it. The collision disconnected the tiller—the heavy iron bar that holds the rudder to the steering wheel. The free-swinging tiller slammed into Robert Peary, fracturing his leg.

Peary was carried down to his quarters in intense pain. Dr. Cook put a splint on Peary's leg and asked Henson to build a wooden box that could serve as a cast.[6] Henson's design was a clever one: The box had a small hinged door that could be opened for dressing or cleaning the wound. Peary was forced to stay in his cabin for the next two weeks. Determined that the expedition continue as planned, Peary had a compass installed near his bed so that he could keep watch on the ship's course.[7] The ship was repaired and reached its destination on the northwestern coast by the end of July.

Just two days after anchoring in McCormick Bay, the *Kite* sailed back to the United States. It would not return for a full year. The seven members of the expedition were left in this remote part of the world to fend for themselves.

While Peary continued to recuperate, Henson kept very busy. He turned his attention first to the construction of a house for the coming winter. The group had sailed north in the summer for the simple reason that the sea was navigable only in warm weather. Yet the sunless winter months ahead would make any ice crossing impossible. Peary hoped that his team would adjust to the climate of the region and be ready for action in the spring.

Henson was given plans for a winter cabin that the group named Red Cliff House, after the red cliffs of sandstone found there. Henson constructed a two-room house that was twenty-one feet long by twelve feet wide.[8] Peary and his wife would have one room while the five others shared slightly larger quarters. The roof and walls of the house were covered with tar paper for insulation, and a potbellied coal stove in the center of the house provided heat.[9]

After Henson finished building the house, he began working on the long wooden sleds, called sledges, which the team would use to transport supplies on the ice cap. He used no nails in the sledges' construction since metal could crack in the cold.

Instead, he drilled many holes into the oak sidebars, then wove thick strips of walrus hide through each hole to bind the crosspieces together.[10]

On August 8, Jo Peary made a special dinner for Henson's twenty-fifth birthday. The group sat on packing crates because they had no other furniture. Peary toasted Henson with a drink he nicknamed the Red Cliff cocktail, and the party was a lively one.[11] Henson wrote later: "Never before in my life had the anniversary of my birth been celebrated, and to have a party given in my honor touched me deeply."[12]

With summer at an end, Matt Henson made a final inspection of the base camp. Confident that he had made it ready for winter, he turned next to an important

Henson repairs a sledge that was designed to carry a load of eight hundred pounds.

assignment: establishing ties with the Inuit. No expedition in the Arctic had any hope of succeeding without the help of its native people. Henson enjoyed a natural advantage over the others.

Henson's brown skin led the native people to believe he was one of their own. At that time, the Inuit people of Greenland, Alaska, and the Canadian Arctic were known as Eskimos. In their language, the word is Inuit. Matt Henson was greeted again and again with the excited welcome of "Inuit! Inuit!" Even though Henson explained that he was not Inuit, he became the American that the Inuit held in greatest esteem.[13]

Through his daily contact, Matt Henson quickly began learning to speak the Inuit language. On this and all future expeditions, Henson was the only American in the group who could communicate well with the Inuit in their own language. The greeting *Hi-nay-nuk-who-nay* asked "How are you?" *Ah-ee-who-ghia* was the response "I am fine." *I-du-di-ah* meant iceberg; *kang-wah-chee* were binoculars.[14] The language is not complex, and Henson could speak it in just a few months.

Henson felt a deep bond with the Inuit. He wrote:

> Many and many a time, for periods covering more than twelve months, I have been to all intents an Esquimo, with Esquimos for companions, speaking their language, dressing in the same kind of clothes, living in the same kind of dens, eating the same food,

Henson formed a close bond with the Inuit: "I have come to love these people. I know every man, woman, and child in their tribe."

enjoying their pleasures, and frequently sharing their griefs. I have come to love these people. I know every man, woman, and child in their tribe. They are my friends and they regard me as theirs.[15]

The Inuit felt similarly toward Henson. They called him *Mahri-Pahluk*, which meant "Matthew the Kind One."[16] Ootah, one of the four Inuit who would go with Henson to the North Pole, said this:

> If it had not been for Mahri-Pahluk, Peary might have been quite another man. Mahri-Pahluk was the only man . . . who could learn to talk our language without using his tongue like a baby. . . . Mahri-Pahluk showed all his days that he did not look down upon people from up here. . . . he wanted to learn our ways and he sure did. . . . we will always tell our children about him and we will sing songs about him.[17]

Henson's special relationship with the Inuit was very important for the Peary expeditions. The Inuit viewed Robert Peary as their employer; they trusted Henson as a friend. The Inuit who accompanied the team in its quest for the North Pole would not have done so if not for Matt Henson.[18]

In the first weeks of winter, the Inuit began teaching Henson the skills he would need to survive in the Arctic. The first lessons concentrated on protection from the extreme cold. Henson learned to cut snow blocks to build an igloo. He was taught to insulate his sealskin boots with moss. If his feet still were very cold, the Inuit warmed them against their bare stomachs.[19] Because of the cold, he was told never to remove the fur clothing the Inuit women had sewn for him. The women had chewed on the skins for many hours to soften them, resting their jaws every other day.[20]

Henson learned to hunt seal, walrus, hare, reindeer, bear, and musk oxen. Though he had a rifle, the Inuit showed him how to use a harpoon. Seal hunting required patience. An Inuit hunter might sit on an ice block for hours waiting for a single seal to surface for air. Walruses were easier to find but harder to kill. Walrus hide is so thick that a harpoon spear, or even a bullet, only wounds the animal. The Inuit showed Henson how to attach a long line with a seal bladder float to his spear and let the harpooned walrus swim with the boat until it tired.[21]

The most important thing Matt Henson learned from the Inuit was how to drive a dog team. On a typical sledge, eight dogs pulled, each one tethered to a fifteen-foot leash called a trace. The traces were brought together by a crosspiece called a toggle that the driver controlled with one hand while cracking a thirty-foot whip with the other. Used correctly, the whip would not actually touch the dogs but snap just above their heads.

Driving was very difficult to learn and to do well. It took Henson many hours of practice before he was able to control the whip and dogs. The first time Henson tried to drive the sledge, his Inuit teachers laughed as he "cracked the long whip everywhere but

The Inuit trusted Henson as a friend. The women sewed fur garments to protect him from the bone-chilling Arctic cold.

where he should . . . showered the dogs with snow . . . [and] tangled himself up in the thirty-foot lash, while the dogs, bored by the performance, sat on their haunches and wondered what was expected of them."[22]

After that comical start though, Henson rapidly learned the skill. The Inuit taught him to find the most aggressive dog and let it lead the pack. With the lead dog up front, the others would follow, even when it meant jumping over open water. Henson's Inuit teachers showed him how to control the twelve-foot sledge over ice and advised him that when the snow became too deep he had to get off and push.[23]

Matt Henson became a masterful sledge driver. Peary said that Henson could "handle a sledge better, and is probably a better dog-driver, than any other man living, except some of the best Eskimo hunters themselves."[24] Henson's skill with the sledge would be of enormous value to Peary during their time in the North.

This first winter in the Arctic (1891–1892) was a tough one for Henson and the others. The polar region tilts on the earth's axis at a sharp angle away from the sun. The sun appears only as a dim glow on the southern horizon. It never rises, and a day has no clear beginning. For months, daylight is a misty twilight that continues into night. With the normal rhythm of day and night missing, the team felt continually gloomy and out of sorts.

The first time Henson tried to drive a dog team, the Inuit laughed at his clumsiness and the dogs gave him bored stares. But he quickly mastered this difficult skill.

Beginning in mid-October, Henson and the other expedition members had to adjust to a world without sunlight. Though they had tried to prepare themselves for it, the certainty of the constant darkness was hard to bear. Even the native Inuit were not immune to this depression. They had a word for it, *perlerorneq*, which means feeling "the weight of life."[25]

The sun returned in February and lifted the spirits of the group. Now the crew could focus on their reason for coming North in the first place. Peary's leg had healed, and he began to put plans into motion. The men traveled to the base of the ice cap with provisions like tea, condensed milk, and tinned pemmican. The supplies were deposited at strategic sites called caches. The men marked each cache with a pole so that they would be able to find it again.

The sledges were loaded with scientific field equipment. There were chronometers to measure time, thermometers and barometers to measure weather conditions, a sextant and artificial horizon to measure altitude and latitudinal position, and compasses to determine direction.[26]

The Inuit at the camp were leery about climbing the glacier. They feared the evil spirit they called *Tornarsuk* would bring harm to anyone who ventured out onto the ice cap. Why travel so far from home, so far from known food sources? they wondered. A person who would act so foolishly would surely anger *Tornarsuk*.[27] The Inuit warned Henson to be careful of crevasses, deep craggy holes in the ice that could trap and kill a man.

Severe storms kept delaying the team's departure. Finally, in late April, they began the steep climb up the glacier's side. It took until the middle of May to get all the supplies onto the ice cap. At this point, Peary decided that things would be speeded up if only he and Eivind Astrup tried the crossing. Henson and the others returned to base camp.

The group waited at Red Cliff house for weeks with no word from Peary. In July, the *Kite* arrived to take the expedition home. The ship would be able to navigate freely for only the next few weeks. But Peary and

Constant dangers threatened the explorers' lives. Peary warned that one swipe of a polar bear's paw could crush a man's head "like an eggshell."

Astrup's whereabouts were still unknown. A rescue party led by Henson was just about to begin a search when the two men returned.

Though weakened by hunger and fatigue, the travelers were jubilant. Robert Peary reported that they had skied and sledded their way across the ice cap on a northeasterly route four hundred miles from camp. They had arrived at cliffs more than three thousand feet above a large body of water. Peary suspected that this water was a bay and named it Independence Bay. North of the bay was an open plain of snow.

Peary had good reason to hope that the water was a bay and not merely a fjord, or narrow inlet. The existence of a bay would prove that Greenland was an island, something mapmakers had wanted to know for centuries. This discovery would make Peary famous. And if Independence Bay marked the northern border of Greenland, then the open plain on the other side might lead to the biggest prize of all—the North Pole.

The crew was ready to sail south in the *Kite* when John Verhoeff disappeared. He had gone on a two-day hike to collect rock specimens, but he did not return. For five days Henson led the group looking for him. When Captain Pike insisted the ship must sail, four hundred pounds of provisions were left for Verhoeff, though the Inuit were certain he had been taken by *Tornarsuk*. Verhoeff was never found, and he is presumed to have died from a fall into a crevasse.[28] In his original letter to Peary, Verhoeff had predicted that he would die; his suspicion had come true.

Except for the disappearance of John Verhoeff, the North Greenland expedition of 1891–1892 was considered a great success. Very soon after their return to the United States, Peary and Henson set to work raising the money they would need for their next trip.

5

"THE LONG RACE WITH DEATH"

A very large and fancy dinner was held to celebrate the success of the North Greenland Expedition. Twelve hundred people came to the Philadelphia Academy of Natural Sciences to honor Robert Peary and his wife.[1] Matt Henson was not invited to the party. This was one of many times that Henson's efforts on Peary's behalf would go unnoticed.

Henson was in Brooklyn, New York, recuperating from temporary sun blindness. The fierce Arctic sun had damaged the iris in one of his eyes despite the protective goggles he had worn. Dr. Frederick Cook, the surgeon on the Greenland trip, had arranged for Henson to see an eye specialist. The long separation had not been good for Henson's marriage, and he stayed at Cook's house while recovering from treatment.

The newspapers and geographic societies were calling Peary a hero.[2] Even Fridtjof Nansen, the Norwegian who had crossed the ice cap before him, wrote a letter of congratulations.[3] With such public approval, Peary managed to get another leave authorized by the navy. Now all he needed was to raise some money.

Peary hoped to return to Greenland within six months. Nansen may have signed his letter "Your admirer," but Peary fretted that his Norwegian rival was already plotting his next move in the race to the Pole. Peary planned a series of lectures about his expedition that he hoped would entice listeners to support another one.

Matt Henson joined Peary for the speaking tour. They used sledges, harpoons, and snowshoes as props to make the lecture halls look like the Arctic. Peary narrated a slide show while Henson, perspiring in a fur parka and boots, brought six barking sled dogs onstage. In three months they gave their talk 165 times and earned enough to pay for another voyage.[4] In the audience of a lecture in Philadelphia, Henson spotted the navy officer who had bet $100 that Henson could not endure the Arctic cold. Waving healthy fingers and toes, Henson gleefully took his money.[5]

The Second Greenland Expedition sailed down the Delaware River from Philadelphia on June 26, 1893. The *Falcon*, a black-hulled ship with three yellow masts, made stops in Brooklyn, Boston, and Portland, Maine, while crowds of people paid twenty-five cents each to come on board and cheer its crew.

There was a large crew aboard. Besides Peary and Henson, there were eleven other men. Except for Eivind Astrup, none of the others had been to the Arctic before. Dr. Cook had decided at the last minute not to join the group, and a surgeon named Edwin Vincent replaced him. Josephine Peary again accompanied her husband, but as this trip set sail, she was six months pregnant. With Mrs. Peary was a nurse who would help deliver and take care of the baby.

Robert Peary insisted that all who came on the journey sign a contract promising not to lecture or write about it afterward. Peary wanted to be able to raise money for future expeditions through his own speaking tours and books. The contract also stated that Peary was the sole commander of the expedition and that all who joined him were expected to "loyally aid and support" him.[6]

The *Falcon* made stops for coal and for sled dogs. On August 3 it moored at Bowdoin Bay, an inlet in southern Greenland named by Peary after his college

Bundled in furs, Peary readies himself on the back of the sledge.

in Maine. Within a day of landing, Matt Henson began
building the much larger house the expedition would
require this time at the base camp. Since Peary and his
wife had celebrated their wedding anniversary at this
location a year earlier, they called this house
Anniversary Lodge.

Robert and Josephine Peary soon had more to celebrate. A daughter, Marie Ahnighito Peary, was born
on September 12. The Inuit were amazed by her
pale skin and gently touched it to assure themselves
that the baby was real and not made of snow. From the
day of her birth, Marie was nicknamed the "Snow
Baby."[7]

Henson finished the house and turned to building
sledges. Peary wanted to get a large cache of supplies
as far out on the ice cap as possible before winter.
Henson readied the sledges with provisions, and
Astrup and another man took off. A week later some
Inuit ran into camp to report that a storm had trapped
the two men halfway up the glacier wall. Henson and
Peary left at once to assist them.

While they were gone, an emergency occurred at
the base camp. An iceberg broke off from the glacier
and fell into the ocean. The weight of its fall created a
massive wave, which flooded the camp. Three boats
were wrecked and some barrels of fuel needed for the
expedition were swept out to sea.

Henson and Peary soon returned with the missing

men, who were hurt but not seriously. Despite their own exhaustion after the rescue mission, Henson and Peary spent the next twenty-four hours in and out of the icy water recovering fuel drums. This difficult and troubled start to the expedition was not a good sign.

The first week of March brought the crew out onto the ice cap eager to begin the crossing. The group included Peary, Henson, six other men from the team, and five Inuit. They would travel with twelve fully loaded sledges and more than ninety sled dogs. Henson privately worried that the traveling party was too large.[8] He believed that a smaller group could travel with greater speed and efficiency.

The Second Greenland Expedition, like the first,

One of the first steps in setting up camp for the night was to cut blocks of snow for building igloos.

was not to be a success. For five weeks the team battled continuous storms with bitter cold and high winds. Many of the dogs froze to death or went mad with *piblokto,* a disease common to dogs in the Arctic (it is similar to rabies). A number of the men got frostbite on their hands or feet. Peary described the grave conditions during one of the storms:

> The straining and flapping of the tent, the deafening roar of the wind, the devilish hissing of the drift, the howling and screaming of the poor dogs, made a pandemonium never to be forgotten . . . for thirty-four hours the average wind velocity had been over forty-eight miles per hour, and the average temperature about minus 50 degrees.[9]

On April 10, they had traveled only 128 miles from their starting point. Robert Peary gave the crew orders to turn back. He instructed them to unload provisions along the route, leaving caches. Each cache was marked with a nine-foot pole. Peary felt certain that he would be able to locate the provisions and use them on a future mission.

When the men got back to Anniversary Lodge, Henson assisted Dr. Vincent, who prescribed what he could for the sick and frostbitten crew. Having never once removed their furs during the trek, the men also were infested with body lice. For two weeks, the base camp was transformed into a makeshift hospital.

While concerned for the welfare of his crew, Robert Peary was concerned also that the mission's failure would bring an end to the financial support he needed. The *Falcon* was returning in August. Word of his defeat would be brought back with the ship. Peary wanted to do something before then that would persuade his backers to finance another expedition.

Peary had heard reports of the existence of strange "iron mountains," which he believed were likely to be meteorites.[10] A young man named Hugh Lee and an Inuit guide ventured south with Peary in search of these geological oddities. Near Melville Bay they found three enormous meteorites. One was shaped like a dog, one had a female form, and the third and largest by far looked like a tent. Peary scratched a "P" on the rock that looked like a woman and made plans to return for them all at a later date.[11]

Peary hoped that news of the meteorites would be important to scientists in the United States. He had little else in the way of success to report. Though he had not intended to do so, Peary saw no alternative to staying in Greenland for the winter and attempting another crossing of the ice cap in the spring. He was uncertain that he would be able to persuade anyone to stay with him.

The *Falcon* left Bowdoin Bay in late August on its return voyage, but every man except Matt Henson and Hugh Lee went with it. To protect her baby's health, Josephine Peary went home, too. Only Henson and Lee had the nerve to stay north for another year.

It would take lots of muscle and even greater ingenuity to bring this seventy-thousand-pound meteorite back to the United States.

For Henson, deciding to stay was easy. Finding meaningful work in the United States had proved very hard for him. With Peary, Henson was assured of adventure, travel, and important work. While the winter would be difficult, Henson knew he had an essential role with the polar team. He wrote that "I have been a member of every expedition of his, in the capacity of assistant: a term that covers a multitude of duties, abilities, and responsibilities."[12]

Henson's immediate responsibility after the boat left was to obtain a winter supply of meat. The *Falcon* had not brought any extra supplies north because the entire expedition had been expected to go back with it. For two months, Matt Henson and an Inuit assistant hunted for walrus, reindeer, and seal.

In October, Henson and Hugh Lee went to check on the caches they had left nearest the base camp. What they found horrified them: The nine-foot-tall pole markers were just barely poking out of the snow. All the provisions they had counted on to carry them through the winter were buried beyond reach in the frozen ground. The men were stranded with the barest of resources.

The game that Henson brought home was their only food. His Inuit friends warned him that the lost caches were signs of an angry *Tornarsuk*. Henson kept hunting throughout the winter months, venturing out most often at night under moonlight.

The three men survived what Peary described as a "nightmare" of a winter.[13] On the morning of April 1, 1895, they left Anniversary Lodge for another test on the Greenland ice. They planned to cross just to the south of the path taken by Peary and Astrup. The night before, the trio had taken baths, shaved, and cut their hair short in an effort to ward off lice. They had also each written letters which they left to be read in the event of their deaths.[14]

It was a particularly risky trip this time. Unless they found reindeer or musk oxen on the barren ice before their limited supply of walrus meat ran out, they would die of starvation. Because they were carrying meat instead of the much lighter dried pemmican that was in their caches, their sledges were overloaded. The Inuit could not be persuaded to stay with them. Henson, Lee, and Peary were on their own.

In the end they would stand on the cliffs of Independence Bay and still be no closer to determining whether Greenland was an island and whether the land to the north was the Pole. The return trip would almost kill them all. Henson said later that of all of his memories of the Arctic "the recollections of the long race with death across the 450 miles of the ice-cap of North Greenland in 1895 . . . are still the most vivid."[15]

Hugh Lee became sick at the very beginning of the trip and had to ride much of the way on Henson's sledge. All three men were weakened by the frozen walrus meat, which cut their mouths and wreaked havoc with their stomachs. After four weeks the food supply was so low they could not afford to share with the dogs. Henson had to begin killing the weakest dogs and feeding them to the dogs who were still able to haul.

The men were down to the end of their rations when Henson came upon a herd of musk oxen. He shot and skinned the animals and the men fell upon the carcasses, eating the meat raw. By the time they reached Independence Bay a few days later, the men were too frail and tired to climb down the nearly-four-thousand-foot cliffs to explore.

The musk ox meat ran out halfway back. For two hundred miles the men trudged on with almost nothing to eat. Only one dog survived, and it was too weak to pull: Hugh Lee was carried on a sledge pulled by Henson and Peary. Henson guided them back to camp and the men collapsed in their bunks at Anniversary Lodge.

For days they lingered near death. The men had scurvy, a disease caused by the lack of vitamin C in their diet. The scurvy brought on massive swelling in their legs and black rot in their gums. Their teeth hung loosely by the roots.[16] Henson had lost fifty pounds—a third of his body weight—and his bones protruded grotesquely.

The three Americans were saved by the traditional Inuit ways.[17] An Inuit woman lay next to Henson for hours, warming him with her body heat. Henson drank seal's blood, a common Inuit medicine. The Inuit shaman, or spiritual leader, danced and chanted in a further effort to restore the men's health.

The men survived, but again their journey had proved futile. To have something to show for two years in the Arctic, Peary resolved to bring the meteorites back. When the *Kite* came to fetch the men, Peary had the ship stop for the massive stones. As an engineer he could estimate their weight and knew that only the two smaller meteorites could be hoisted on board; at 1,000 and 5,500 pounds each they were heavy enough, but the tent-shaped rock weighed nearly 70,000 pounds.[18]

Robert Peary hoped the meteorites would impress the funders back home.[19] Despite the near-death experience, he was certain that the North Pole could be reached. Matt Henson had shown that he was the equal of any man who had challenged the Arctic. The two men would figure out some way to get to the Pole— and before anyone else beat them to it.

6

MARATHON

Matthew Henson, Robert Peary, and Hugh Lee returned to the United States to find that the competition to reach the North Pole had heated up considerably in their absence. Fridtjof Nansen had set a new world record for Farthest North, coming within 230 miles of the Pole on an unusual ship designed to drift with the ice floes. A Swedish engineer was considering flying to the Pole in a balloon filled with hydrogen.

If they wanted to win the race to the North Pole, Henson and Peary had to act quickly. They had to put the terrible hardships of the failed Second Greenland

Expedition behind them and move forward. They gave the two meteorites to the American Museum of Natural History in New York City. The meteorite exhibit drew large crowds and impressed scientists.[1] The money required for another voyage seemed assured.

Matt Henson was offered a job at the same museum. A curator there had seen the mounted walrus and musk oxen the expedition had brought back and admired Henson's skill at animal skinning.[2] At the Museum of Natural History, Henson assisted with mounting the animals and creating authentic Arctic scenes for the displays.

While he was in New York City, two things had a profound effect on Henson's personal life. The first was a divorce from his wife, Eva. The marriage simply could not survive Henson's constant time away.[3] The second was that Henson became part of a circle of African Americans who viewed his role with Robert Peary as inspirational to their race. Prominent among these new friends was a man named George Gardner. Gardner urged Henson to do all he could to reach the Pole alongside Peary and give black Americans a new national hero.[4]

Peary soon asked Henson to take a leave from his museum job and help bring the largest of the meteorites back from Greenland. It took the men two separate trips, one in 1896 and another the following year, before they were able to free the massive rock and get it home. The seventy-thousand-pound specimen from outer space was given the name "Ahnighito" and added to the Museum of Natural History's permanent collection.

Peary now felt that he could focus all his energies on getting to the North Pole. He had just received medals from two important geographic societies. The newly formed Peary Arctic Club, a group of wealthy businessmen under the leadership of Morris K. Jesup, had promised to "see him through" another voyage.[5] Peary decided that on this journey north he would limit his traveling companions to two men—Matt Henson and Thomas Dedrick, a doctor from New Jersey.

Interest in the polar exploration team was keen both in the United States and overseas. The publisher of the *Daily Mail*, a major London newspaper, made a gift of a ship to the expedition.[6] This ship, the *Windward*, was once used by Fridtjof Nansen. The expedition set off in July 1898.

Peary planned this time to sail farther up the Greenland coast than he had previously. He figured that if he could anchor farther north, the group would have fewer miles to sledge. Once again, the expedition did not start off according to plans. The *Windward* soon became trapped in the pack ice off the shore of Ellesmere Island, far south of the planned landing site

Henson and Peary aboard the *Windward.* The ship was a gift from a London newspaper publisher.

and fully seven hundred miles from the Pole. The men were forced to unload the ship and begin sledging 250 miles to Fort Conger, the same base camp from which the Greely expedition had hoped to be rescued fifteen years earlier.

Matt Henson and four Inuit assistants went ahead to cut the trail. Ellesmere Island is just a short way across the channel from Greenland, but its terrain is wilder. The Inuit call it *oomingmannuna*, the musk oxen's country.[7] On the ice cap in Greenland the ground felt solid; on Ellesmere Island, the ocean rolled unpredictably beneath the ice. Pressure ridges caused by colliding ice blocks below the surface made the ground open up unexpectedly. Henson had to be on the lookout at all times for open water, which could drown him.

The trail cutting was complicated further by the fact that it was already winter. The sun had set for the season and the temperature was fifty degrees below zero. Under the glow of the moon Henson pushed the loaded sledges northward, building igloos for shelter. Peary and Dedrick followed his jagged path and eventually caught up. The last part of their journey was the most treacherous—it took place in complete darkness.

Like blind men they groped their way along the coastline, actually picking up and carrying the heavy sledges at the points where the ice was most broken. The raw wind slapped at them ferociously and the cold killed two dogs. The men did not sleep for nearly a week. On January 6, 1899, they somehow found the abandoned Fort Conger.

It was an eerie place: The Greely camp had been preserved intact by the extreme cold. It was if the men had stepped back fifteen years in time. Peary described the scene in his diary:

> In the men's quarters dishes remained on the table just as left after lunch or dinner of the day when the fort was deserted. Biscuits were scattered in every direction, overturned cups, etc., seemed to give indications of a hasty departure. To my surprise, the biscuits on the table, though somewhat tough, were not mouldy or

Extraordinary strength was needed to move the sledges over the jagged mountains of snow and ice.

spoiled. . . . Coffee in the bottom of one of the tins . . . was found to have sufficient strength that by using a double amount, drinkable coffee could be made. After some considerable delay, owing to difficulty in making the range draw, we were all enjoying an ad lib supply of coffee and biscuits.[8]

That the food was edible was a stroke of good luck; the men's rations had run out two days before and they had been forced to kill a dog for food. But their luck turned in the next few hours. Peary discovered that his toes were frostbitten. When his frozen boots were pried off, several toes on each foot broke off at the joints. Henson knew that Peary's circulation must be restored or a disease called gangrene would kill him. If the remaining toes could not be saved, they would have to be amputated.

Dr. Dedrick had with him at Fort Conger only the most primitive tools and medicine. His medical bag had been left on the *Windward*. For six weeks Peary lay in bed with no painkiller, unable to walk. Henson hunted musk oxen to eat. In mid-February he strapped Peary onto a sledge and with Dedrick drove the 250 miles back to the ship. There the doctor cut off all but two of Peary's toes.

Despite the amputation, Robert Peary resolved to stay in the Arctic. The *Windward* finally broke free of the ice by late summer and the crew sailed a short way south to Etah, an Inuit settlement in northern Greenland. The men would winter here and return to

Fort Conger in the spring. While in Etah, Peary got news from the United States that he had another daughter. She had been born on the same January night that he had lost his toes.

In April 1900, Matt Henson and Robert Peary set out to determine once and for all whether Greenland was an island. Thomas Dedrick remained at Fort Conger to hunt. Henson and Peary trekked hundreds of miles along the icy cliffs of the bleak north coast. The going was particularly difficult for Peary with his nearly toeless feet. Yet by the third week in May, the men knew for certain that Greenland was an island. An accurate map of the country could be drawn for the first time.

Henson and Peary's mapping of the previously uncharted territory of Greenland was an important contribution to geography. Knowing that Greenland was an island confirmed that the only route to the North Pole was across the dangerous, fast-moving pack ice of the Arctic Ocean. This ice is what makes the North Pole much more difficult to reach than the South Pole, which is on land. Peary and Henson decided that their next attempt at the North Pole would start from the channel between Greenland and Ellesmere Island. This approach to the Pole later became known as the American Route.[9]

Henson, Peary, and Dedrick remained at Fort Conger for the next ten months. The purple heather and blue anemones that dotted the tundra for a short spell in the summer soon gave way to the absolute white of winter. The sun disappeared and the temperature dropped sharply. The small Arctic animals—fox, hare, lemming, and ptarmigan—were camouflaged.

The game in the region was plentiful. Henson hunted musk oxen, killing more than one hundred of them on a single trip. He bagged hare by the dozens.

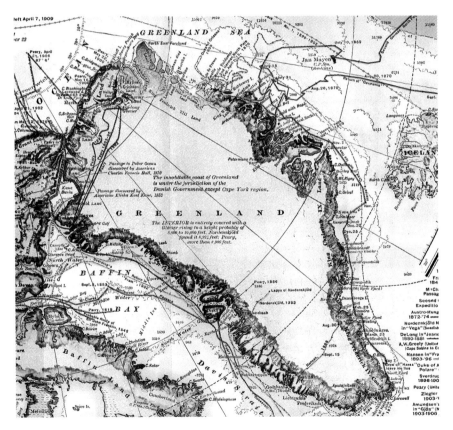

Thanks to Henson and Peary, accurate maps of Greenland could be drawn for the first time.

He was able to fish for Atlantic salmon with his bare hands.[10]

Holed up in base camp, the men did not know that 250 miles to the south and locked in the ice was a ship crowded with people anxious to see them. Upon hearing of her husband's frostbite injuries, Josephine Peary had hired the boat and sailed north with a group including their seven-year-old daughter, Marie. The Peary's baby daughter, Francene, had died of the disease cholera the month before.

In early April, Henson and Peary began a march on the ice that ended a mere eight days later when weather conditions made further travel impossible. Back at Fort Conger the men were met by a group from Jo Peary's ship. The Pearys were reunited for the summer, and Peary first learned the sad news of his daughter's death and also that of his mother.

Josephine and Marie Peary sailed home in August leaving Peary, Henson, and Dedrick for one more winter. Though he was determined to make another attempt at the Pole, Peary was saddened by the separation from his family.

Matt Henson too was affected by the visitors from the United States.[11] Henson was aware that the life he had waiting for him upon his return to the United States was very different from Peary's. There he had no family and quite possibly no job. In many ways, despite the physical hardships, Matt Henson's life in the Arctic was better than his life at home.

Henson and Peary were about to begin their fourth consecutive year in the Arctic. Dr. Dedrick had finally had enough and submitted his resignation. He went to live for a year in an Inuit village, causing Peary to worry that the doctor might make his own run at the Pole.[12] Henson and Peary would make the next trek alone. They spent the fall and winter hunting and moving caches in preparation for the spring.

Their Inuit assistants were not healthy. A stomach ailment had infected all of them in the camp and they believed that *Tornarsuk* was behind it.[13] As the time for the journey neared, the Inuit refused to help load the sledges. Speaking in their language, Henson reassured them.[14] Were it not for their trust of Henson, it is doubtful that the Inuit would have agreed to leave the base camp.

As it turned out, the four-hundred-mile trek, which began March 24, 1902, ended without much success a month later. It really did seem that an evil spirit was alive in the polar sea. The ice cap moved constantly, rising up and groaning with what Henson described as "an almost ear-splitting" sound.[15] Ice floes of all sizes floated in the inky water.

With no warning, the heaving ice cracked and formed leads—rivers of open water. If the lead was a narrow one, the dogs could jump it or Henson might unleash them and use the sledge as a small bridge. Sometimes the lead was much wider and the men and dogs would be forced to stop and double-back in their tracks, or simply wait hours in the cold for the water to refreeze.

On April 21, the men were stopped by a lead more than a mile across.[16] Their supplies had dwindled so low that they could not risk waiting for the sea to freeze. They had reached a new American record for Farthest North at 84 degrees 16 minutes north latitude.[17] But they could travel no further. It was time for Henson to lead them back.

Henson later wrote:

> During the four years from 1898 to 1902, which were continuously spent in the regions about North Greenland, we had every experience, except death, that had ever fallen to the lot of explorers who had preceded us, and more than once we looked death squarely in the face.[18]

It is hard to imagine the brutal marathon of four straight years in the Arctic. Though Henson and Peary had not accomplished what they had most hoped, they had survived an ordeal that would have killed lesser men. And they had cemented a partnership. The men sailed back to the United States in August 1902. They would need time to recoup, but they would most certainly be back.

7

FARTHEST NORTH

obert Peary and Matthew Henson were not the only explorers who had recently returned after four years in the Arctic. A Norwegian, Otto Sverdrup, had spent the same four years exploring Ellesmere Island and many smaller islands to the west.[1] Sverdrup had served as captain to Fridtjof Nansen, and he took Nansen's smooth-bottomed ship, the *Fram*, on his voyage. Peary had tried to keep informed of Sverdup's whereabouts, worrying that he might at any moment turn north and make a beeline for the Pole.[2]

There were many who believed that Peary should

be honored for his efforts of the past four years even though the expedition did not reach the North Pole. He received medals from the American, French, and Scottish geographical societies.[3] The navy promoted him to the level of commander.[4] Once again, Henson received no recognition of any kind for his contributions.

Henson had not been paid a salary by Peary either, and now that he was back in the United States, he had to make some money. He took a job as a porter with the Pennsylvania Railroad. Train travel at that time was very popular, and travelers slept overnight in railway cars called Pullman sleepers. Henson carried baggage and made up the sleeping berths for the passengers on these cars.

With his love of travel, the job of Pullman porter seemed ideal at first to Matt Henson.[5] He knew that it would be some time before Peary had raised enough money to finance another trip. Henson had never before been anywhere in the United States other than some cities in the North East. For six months he traveled throughout New England and the Midwest.

Henson enjoyed his new job until he decided to take an assignment on a train bound for the South. The palm trees and fruit orchards of Florida had intrigued him.[6] Then an attempt on his life by racist men with shotguns quickly made him lose all interest. The men attacked Henson early one morning, shouting racial slurs and throwing oranges. When night fell,

Because he was African American, Henson received no medals or honors after his four-year Arctic exploration.

the men returned with guns. A shotgun blast missed Henson, shattering the glass in the Pullman car instead, but the rage of his attackers was enough to convince him that the South was an intolerant place.[7]

Matt Henson had faced prejudice many times before in his life, but attempted murder was something else entirely. He was understandably shaken by the incident. Henson had become accustomed to a world in which white, black, and Inuit worked together.[8] In the Arctic he did not experience the open bigotry that he faced in America. In the Arctic, the issue of survival was much more important than the issue of race. It was a simple fact that every man had to treat others as brothers or risk death.

Henson soon quit his porter's job and returned to New York City. His friend George Gardner welcomed him back, and at a dinner party at Gardner's home, Henson met a young woman, Lucy Jane Ross. In a short time, they fell in love and became engaged to be married. Henson confessed that he had little in the way of money to offer, but he promised to give Lucy Ross a large wedding gift—the North Pole![9]

Henson had by this time heard from Robert Peary that a fifth expedition to the Pole was being planned.* The Peary Arctic Club had sponsored the manufacture of a steamship, the *Roosevelt*, with one-thousand-horse-power engines.[10] The ship was named after President

---

*Editor's note: This expedition was described briefly in Chapter 1.

Theodore Roosevelt, one of the expedition's most enthusiastic supporters.

President Roosevelt was himself an avid hunter and sportsman and had been following the accomplishments of the polar team long before he became president. He was in fact a member of the Peary Arctic Club. After the last trek, Roosevelt's signature headlined a congratulatory letter sent to the crew which read, in part:

> It [the Club] honors you for patience, courage and fortitude, undaunted by formidable obstacles; thanks you for the wise and effective use of the means placed at your disposal, and congratulates you upon your achievements memorable in the annals of science and discovery.[11]

Arctic explorers were the kind of gutsy physical personalities that Roosevelt most admired. He also looked forward to the prestige that would be associated with the United States if the group were the first to reach the Pole. With Theodore Roosevelt as president, Robert Peary's money worries appeared over. Just as important, Peary no longer had to be concerned about the navy's granting him leave.[12]

The *Roosevelt* was due to set sail in July 1905. Henson visited the site where the boat was being built and was impressed with the ship's construction.[13] It was not a large ship, but it was a strong one, with oak and steel cross-braces in its frame. The *Roosevelt* was narrow

The *Roosevelt* was not a large ship, but it was specially designed for the icy Arctic waters.

in the front to help cut through the ice, and wider on the bottom to help keep the ice from crushing it.

The team for this voyage included Louis Wolf, a surgeon from Oregon; and Ross Marvin, a science professor from Cornell University. Both men were thirty years old—ten years younger than Henson and twenty years younger than Peary. The other two men on board were the steward, Charles Percy, and the ship's captain, Robert Bartlett, a seasoned navigator from Newfoundland.

The *Roosevelt* steamed north from New York through the Gulf of St. Lawrence and up the coast of Labrador. Its first stop was Etah, an Inuit settlement in Greenland. In Etah the ship was loaded with tons of coal for fuel, tons of whale and walrus meat for food, and 130 dogs for pulling the sleds.[14] From Etah the crowded ship wedged its way farther north through the icy waters.

Captain Bartlett steered the ship from a high perch in the crow's nest. He shouted commands down to Henson and the other crew members, straining to be heard over the howl of the wind and the incessant barking of the chained sled dogs.[15] After eighteen days and many forced detours, the ship landed at Cape Sheridan, on Ellesmere Island just north of Fort Conger.

The strength of the *Roosevelt*'s design was tested soon after anchoring. A giant, jagged ice floe rammed the ship on two sides, squeezing it in a tight grip. The boat's sides shrank inward from the pressure of the floe for a precarious few moments but then popped back out again with enough force to free the ship from the ice. The wider oval-bottomed design of the ship had saved it and its crew from destruction.[16]

The men spent the winter months preparing for the second stage of their journey. They hunted musk oxen and caribou. They rebuilt and packed the sledges. The crew set aside time for pleasure as well: They held snowshoe and sledging races and on Christmas morning opened packages of cigars, chewing gum, and chocolates sent from Maine by Jo Peary.[17] The dark winter passed relatively quickly and Henson felt confident about the group's chances this time.[18]

At the end of February, Robert Peary divided the men and their Inuit assistants into small groups. Henson's group was to go first, cutting the trail and building igloos at regular intervals. Peary would follow him. The other groups would act like a relay team. Every fifty miles one group would relay its supplies forward to the next group, and so on, with the supplies eventually reaching Henson. After sending their supplies to the lead group, the others would then return to base camp.

By the last week in March, all the teams except Henson's and Peary's had returned. Their march continued until it was stopped by the same wide stream of water they had encountered on their previous trek:

the river they called the "Big Lead."[19] For six days they camped at the river's edge waiting for the water to refreeze. Then, just after making the crossing, they were cut off from the supporting relay teams by a blizzard that hid their tracks. Henson's and Peary's teams were now completely on their own.

The explorers were less than two hundred miles from the North Pole, at 87 degrees 6 minutes north latitude. They were farther north than any expedition had ever gone. Yet because they were out of contact with their supply teams, they would run out of food if they went on. Even if they turned back now, they would have almost nothing to eat on the way back to camp.

In 1902 and 1906, the explorers were forced to retreat across the ice when they came to big leads—rivers too wide to cross.

Henson took the lead position on the retreat southward. The men would starve if they had to wait for the Big Lead to freeze over again, so they made the risky decision to cross on a section of thin ice. Each man knew that once he began the crossing, he could not stop for even a second. The glide of his snowshoe must be constant and swift to avoid breaking the thin ice. Somehow every man in the group passed over the Big Lead to safety. Peary wrote afterward:

> It was evident to us all that now was our chance or never, and I gave the word to put on snowshoes and make the attempt. I tied mine on more carefully than I had ever done before. I think every other man did the same, for we felt that a slip or stumble would be fatal. We had already tested the ice and knew it would not support us an instant without snowshoes. . . .
>
> It was the first and only time in all my Arctic work that I felt doubtful as to the outcome, but when near the middle of the lead the toe of my rear kamik [boot] . . . broke through twice in succession, I thought to myself "This is the finish."[20]

The return march across the polar ice cap continued. Their food now entirely gone, the men began killing the weakest dogs and eating them. Sleep was out of the question; they could not afford to take the time. The men dragged forward for days, following the distant mountains they knew to be Greenland. When one morning they came upon a herd of musk oxen and were able to shoot a few, the men fell upon the still-warm animals and devoured the flesh raw.[21]

In the last week of May, after eighty-eight days on the ice, Matt Henson and Robert Peary staggered back into camp. Henson's first biographer described Henson this way:

> He did not feel as though he was the same man. His body was now a gaunt skeleton. . . . He was almost blind from the burning glare of the sun beating down on stark fields of snow. His brown skin, shrunken over his well-formed skull, was seamed and cracked by the wind and cold, like a shriveled, sun-baked hide. His dazed mind was wrapped in a stupor of exhaustion, but he feebly sought the answer of why it had all happened, why they had failed.[22]

To make matters more complicated, while they were gone the *Roosevelt* had sustained serious damage from the ice. Both the rudder and propeller blades were broken, and for a while there was some question as to whether or not the ship could sail.[23] In the end, the trip back to the United States proved maddeningly slow, but the *Roosevelt* entered New York harbor on Christmas Eve 1906.

For the first time after returning from a voyage, Henson had someone waiting eagerly on the dock to greet him. Lucy Ross and Matt Henson were married in September 1907, nine months after he came home. They would have less than a year together before Henson would leave again for the Arctic. But this time he would bring Lucy the wedding present he had promised her.

8

"THE PRIZE OF THREE CENTURIES"

ome pretty eccentric ideas were sent to Robert Peary from people all over the country who thought they could help him make it to the North Pole. "Flying machines" and submarines were popular schemes, along with cars that expertly handled ice. One man suggested laying miles of hose and pumping hot soup through it. An inventor wanted to shoot Peary out of a cannon.[1]

Peary had his own new plan. It was not so different from his old plan, but he had changed the route. His last march had been stymied by the strong flowing current that caused the team to drift off course to the east.

This time, instead of trying to fight the current and forge due north, he planned to cross the polar ice cap in a northwesterly direction and allow the powerful east-flowing currents to help carry him toward the Pole.[2]

The *Roosevelt* had been repaired and refitted with new boilers. The work was largely funded by a donation of $10,000 from a Massachusetts businessman who supported "big things."[3] To the American public and press, reaching the North Pole had become the biggest of stunts, a feat that many believed impossible and gamblers laid long odds against.[4]

Matt Henson spent the months between expeditions supervising the ship's repairs and working on a new sledge design.[5] Henson described the altered sledge with the expertise of a master builder:

> The runners are longer, and are curved upwards at each end, so that they resemble the profile of a canoe, and are expected to rise over the inequalities of the ice much better than the old style. Lashed together with sealskin thongs, about twelve feet long, by two feet wide and seven inches high, the load can be spread along their entire length instead of being piled up, and a more even distribution of the weights is made. The Esquimos, used to their style of sledge, are of the opinion that the new style will prove too much for one man and an ordinary team to handle, but we have given both kinds a fair trial and it looks as if the new type has the old beaten by a good margin.[6]

When the repairs to the ship's machinery had been

completed, the *Roosevelt* was loaded with supplies. For baking, the ship's steward would have on hand sixteen thousand pounds of flour and ten thousand pounds of sugar.[7] The boat's hold was crammed with hundreds of cases of condensed milk, ship's biscuit, canned pemmican, and tins of coffee and tea. Coal, kerosene, dynamite, batteries, and guns filled most of the remaining space below deck. The men's tiny quarters were crowded with their personal belongings and bulky navigational equipment and cameras. Peary's cabin was a little roomier, as was befitting a commander—he even found a corner for a player piano.[8]

On one of the hottest days ever recorded for New York City, the *Roosevelt* sailed north again.[9] It made its first stop at Oyster Bay on Long Island, where Theodore Roosevelt had his summer home. The president wished to give a personal spirited farewell to the group.[10]

The crew for this expedition consisted of men from the previous trip and three newcomers, or "tenderfeet," as Peary called them.[11] The new men had been selected from a long list of young men from all over the United States who had wanted to become part of the world-famous team. The chosen three were George Borup, a recent Yale graduate and track star; Donald MacMillan, a mathematics and physical education teacher; and John Goodsell, who would be the group's doctor.

The *Roosevelt* steamed north to Etah where forty-nine Inuit, including some entire families, joined them. Two hundred forty-six barking sled dogs were brought on board as well. The heavily weighted ship sat low in the water and was ready to depart again when a commotion arose on shore. Matt Henson described the rantings of a desperate man, ". . . the most hopelessly dirty, unkempt, filth-littered human being any of us had ever seen, or could ever have imagined."[12] This man had been exploring with Dr. Frederick Cook, the same Dr. Cook who had been part of Peary's first trip to Greenland.

The crazed man, whose name was Rudolph Franke, had a letter from Cook requesting that Franke be taken back to the United States. Cook was off exploring somewhere in the Arctic. Rudolph Franke was evidence to the Peary team of two things: The first was something they had long suspected—that the brutal life in the Far North could drive a man insane. The second was that Dr. Cook was a serious threat in the competition for the Pole.[13]

Just outside Etah, the *Roosevelt* was hit on two sides by an iceberg. Only one-eighth of an iceberg is visible above the water's surface; the other seven-eighths is hidden under the water, making a safe pass around one difficult.[14]

To free the boat, Captain Bartlett attached sticks of dynamite to a long pole with a wire connecting the

Henson the jaunty sailor stands on the deck of the *Roosevelt* in 1908.

explosives to a battery on board. Bartlett lowered the pole onto the iceberg and the crew ran for cover at a far end of the deck. The dynamite blew the berg wide open, sending water, snow, and ice sky high and releasing the *Roosevelt*.[15]

The *Roosevelt* anchored at Cape Sheridan on September 5, 1908. To commemorate their safe arrival, Robert Peary went to inspect the cairn the group had left three years before. A cairn is a heap of stones piled up as a marker. Explorers leave cairns to provide future missions with useful geographical information about an area, as well as to prove that they were in fact where they claimed to have been. Ross Marvin created the cairn left in 1906, putting papers in a can that had earlier contained prunes.[16]

Matt Henson began at once to instruct the new men on the contrary ways of the Arctic. He taught them how to cut blocks of snow and build an igloo. Once they were proficient with the saw knife, the men could build the snow house in an hour. Henson then told them that if a bad storm blew in they should forget about an igloo for shelter—they would be lucky if they had time to make a dugout in a snow bank. Henson demonstrated the tricks of dogsled driving, explaining that the only solution when the dogs got entangled—which was often—was to take off your gloves and work out the knots with your bare hands.

Over the winter months the young men received a

thorough Arctic education from Matt Henson. By the end of February, all thoughts turned to the mission at hand. For this assault on the Pole, Robert Peary planned to use the same relay system of small groups sending supplies forward to the lead team. Once a group finished its part, it would return to camp. Each man would play a vital role in the total effort, but only the few who accompanied Peary in the last party would actually go to the North Pole. Matt Henson hoped fervently that Peary would again include him in the elite last group.[17]

With eighteen years spent in the region, Henson was without question Robert Peary's most experienced crewman. Together they had set records for Farthest North at 84.16 degrees in 1902 and 87.6 degrees in 1906: Would they reach 90 degrees and stand together at the North Pole this year?

Robert Bartlett was directed to cut the trail for the first marches of this trek. The sun had not yet risen from its winter position below the horizon, so Bartlett attached a lantern to his sledge. The weather was clear, calm, and 50 degrees below zero.[18] Five days later Henson's group caught up with Bartlett's alongside the Big Lead, the river that had delayed their journeys twice before. Peary and MacMillan's teams reached them in the next days and they set up camp together.

The waiting was difficult. The men were anxious to travel in the good weather, but the good weather had

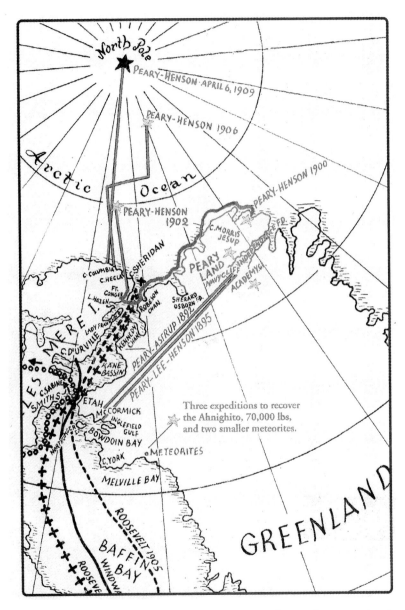

Three expeditions to recover the Ahnighito, 70,000 lbs, and two smaller meteorites.

This map shows the routes of Henson's and Peary's many Arctic expeditions.

actually become a problem in itself. The sun had finally cleared the horizon and the temperature had soared. With temperatures hovering at 20 degrees below zero, it was just too warm for the Big Lead to freeze over. For five days, the men lingered. The Inuit were particularly impatient, and Donald MacMillan created a diversion for many of them by supervising games and races.[19]

On March 11, after seven long days, the river closed up enough for a quick crossing. This was an enormous relief to both Henson and Peary, who knew firsthand that the Big Lead could have ended the expedition. Henson wrote in his diary, "We were sure we had passed the main obstruction,"[20] and Peary later confided in his book that "with memories of the effect of the delay at the 'Big Lead' . . . in the previous expedition. . . . I think that more of mental wear and tear was crowded into those days [of waiting] than into all the rest of the fifteen months we were absent from civilization."[21]

For the next two weeks the men continued the march northward with teams returning to base camp every few days. One of Donald MacMillan's heels became frostbitten, so he was the first to go, with Dr. Goodsell joining him to attend to the injury. George Borup started back next; on the way, he single-handedly saved his dog team from drowning when the sledge slipped between two pieces of floating ice. Ross

Marvin's division was the third to return, leaving only Bartlett, Henson, Peary, and their Inuit assistants.

Matt Henson took on the trailblazing from this point. Since Captain Bartlett had done almost all of the difficult trail cutting until this time, Henson felt strong and rested.[22] He also felt hopeful that he would be asked to cut the last leg to the Pole. Henson later described how he felt when Ross Marvin was sent back: "My heart stopped palpitating, I breathed easier, and my mind was relieved. It was not my turn yet, I was to continue onward and there only remained one person between me and the Pole—the Captain."[23]

During the last week of March, the men traveled fourteen hours every day with a "strong northerly wind blowing full in our faces."[24] On April 1, they were within 150 miles of the North Pole, just short of 88 degrees latitude. It was time for the final assault. Robert Peary directed Captain Bartlett to return to camp. Peary had decided that only Henson and four Inuit—Ootah, Seegloo, Ooqueah, and Egingwah—would join him for the last part of the journey.

Henson and Peary intended to cover the remaining miles over the next five days. This meant that they would need to sledge at the exhausting pace of more than twenty-five miles each day. Matt Henson wrote, "We marched and marched, falling down in our tracks repeatedly, until it was impossible to go on. We were forced to camp, in spite of the impatience of the

Commander, who found himself unable to rest, and who only waited long enough for us to relax into sound sleep, when he would wake us up and start us off again."[25]

On the third day, Henson nearly drowned. While crossing on some moving ice, he fell into a lead. He later described the "instant of hideous horror. . . . I tore my hood from off my head and struggled frantically."[26] Fortunately, within seconds Ootah was able to pull Henson from the freezing water, saving his life.

The rush northward continued. The men worried that as before, something would happen to keep them from the top of the world. Peary's greatest concern was of another lead too wide to cross. He said, "At every inequality of the ice, I found myself hurrying breathlessly forward, fearing that it marked a lead, and when I arrived at the summit would catch my breath with relief—only to find myself hurrying on in the same way at the next one."[27]

In the end they would not come upon a single lead. And in the end, it was Matt and Ootah who got there first. Their sledges arrived at the rubble of snow and ice that Henson reckoned to be the North Pole a full forty-five minutes before Peary. Ever the helpful assistant, Henson began building their shelter while he waited for Peary.[28]

At noon on April 6, 1909, the men took a solar observation with an artificial horizon and a sextant

April 6, 1909, the top of the world at last! From left to right: Ooqueah, Ootah, Henson, Egingwah, Seegloo.

which showed a latitude of 89 degrees 57 minutes.[29] Henson and Peary knew that they could never determine the exact location of 90 degrees north latitude. Although they used the best equipment then available, the frigid conditions caused slight aberrations; 89.57 was within the vicinity of the geographic North Pole. Henson wrote, ". . . while we worked I was nervously apprehensive, for I felt that the end of our journey had come. . . . Another world's accomplishment was done and finished, and as in the past . . . a white man had been accompanied by a colored man."[30]

The men marched back and forth across a ten-mile area, taking additional sun observations and reconfirming their position. Peary placed an American flag in an ice hill and, Henson wrote that as "the glorious banner was unfurled to the breeze, . . . I felt a savage joy and exultation."[31] Peary also took photographs to commemorate the occasion. In one, Henson holds the flag that Josephine Peary had years before made for her husband. The flag is tattered because Peary had left pieces of it in cairns to mark "farthest north" over the years.

The explorers spent thirty hours at the North Pole before they began the trek southward. They still had 450 miles to cover before they could rest. The spring season was upon them and the rising temperature made more likely the emergence of dangerous leads. Matt Henson assumed his familiar position at the front

"I felt a savage joy and exultation," wrote Henson after reaching the North Pole.

of the pack. Doubling back on the trail he had already cut coming north, he guided the party safely to camp in just sixteen days.

This small, brave, multiracial group had reached the North Pole and made it back to tell about it. They were forever changed by their experience. Henson wrote:

> After reaching the land again, I gave a keen searching look at each member of the party, and I realized the strain they had been under. Instead of the plump, round countenances I knew so well, I saw lean, gaunt faces, seamed and wrinkled, the faces of old men, not those of boys, but in their eyes still shone the spark of resolute determination.[32]

Late in July the *Roosevelt* began the voyage home to the United States. The ship retraced its original path, heading south from Cape Sheridan to Etah. Here the Inuit were to leave the ship to be reunited with their families. For Henson this was a difficult and emotional good-bye. He doubted if he would see his friends again. Henson gave his hunting rifle to Ootah as a special gift in thanks for saving his life.[33]

At Etah the men heard disturbing news that clouded the rest of their journey. Frederick Cook had emerged from the Arctic wilderness. He was claiming to have gone to the North Pole a full year before Peary and Henson. The *Roosevelt* was bringing Matt Henson and Robert Peary home to a country that believed it had already welcomed the discoverer of the North Pole.

9

AFTER THE ARCTIC

hough he did not believe that Frederick Cook was telling the truth, Robert Peary was very troubled that others did. Before leaving the Inuit village in Greenland, Peary asked Matt Henson to speak with the Inuit who had traveled with Cook.[1] The Inuit told Henson that they had gone with Cook only a short way off the coast of Ellesmere Island. They had carried few supplies and were always within sight of land. From Henson's conversation, Peary felt certain that Cook had not been anywhere near the North Pole. He immediately telegraphed this information to his wife and *The New York Times*.[2]

Before the polar team had received word of Frederick Cook's claim, they had already dealt with difficult news. Professor Ross Marvin had died on the way back to base camp. The Inuit in his party described his drowning in the icy waters of the Big Lead.[3] It was not until many years later that the truth about Marvin's death was revealed. Ross Marvin was murdered by an Inuit, a man called Harrigan, who shot him because he believed Marvin treated the Inuit unfairly.[4]

On September 21, 1909, the *Roosevelt* steamed into its home port, New York, with an oversized banner that proclaimed "NORTH POLE" waving from one of its masts. A large crowd of people, including reporters from many newspapers, was waiting to greet the expedition. Matt Henson assured a writer from the *New York World* newspaper, "You people needn't worry about Dr. Cook. He's never been to the Pole. Commander Peary and I are the only ones that have ever been there."[5]

For weeks the press enthusiastically covered the story because the controversy helped sell a lot of papers. The very different personalities of the explorers made good copy. Frederick Cook was by all accounts an outgoing and likable man who told one newspaper that he was happy to share the discovery with Peary: "I am proud that a fellow American has

African Americans were thrilled with Henson's role in the discovery of the North Pole.

reached the Pole. . . . There is glory enough for us
all."[6] In contrast, Robert Peary was generally per-
ceived as a poor sport who was interested only in
fame for himself.[7]

The scientific community asked for proof from
both men. Peary submitted his journal and other
records from the expedition and waited tensely at his
home in Maine. From a lecture tour in Europe, Cook
glibly promised he would pull his proof together as
soon as possible and hand it over to scientists in
Denmark.

Cook's proof never appeared. After the University
of Copenhagen disclaimed Cook, the National
Geographic Society gave Peary a special gold medal
and announced that he alone should be credited with
the discovery of the Pole.[8] And based on subsequent
reports from the press and scientific societies, it must
have seemed to the public that Peary had truly acted
alone: Henson's role in the Pole's discovery was for the
most part ignored.

When Henson's assistance was discussed at all, it
was usually questioned. Despite the scientists' findings
that Cook was a fraud, there were many people who
still believed in him. Matt Henson became a favorite
target of Cook's supporters. Peary was asked why he
did not bring Captain Bartlett with him on the final
leg. For those with a racist perspective, and there were

many, Bartlett was presumed to be a more reliable witness than an African American or a native Inuit.

These critics thought that Henson did not have the intellectual ability or the training to confirm Peary's solar observations and claim to the Pole. They were wrong. Matt Henson had learned navigational skills from Ross Marvin, a professor of engineering. He knew how to figure latitude and longitude and was able to confirm the distance landmarks that Peary claimed.[9]

Henson's fellow crewmembers publicly defended him, perhaps none so eloquently as Donald MacMillan, who wrote in *National Geographic* magazine:

> And the negro? He was indispensable to Peary and of more real value than the combined services of all four white men. With years of experience equal to that of Peary himself, an expert dog-driver, a master mechanic, physically strong, most popular with the Eskimos, talking the language like a native, clean full of grit, he went to the Pole with Peary because he was easily the most efficient of all Peary's assistants.[10]

Robert Peary himself said simply, "Henson was the best man I had with me for this kind of work."[11] And he was. Among the Americans, Henson was by a long shot the best sledge driver and most experienced Arctic trekker. He built the shelters and the sledges and the cookstoves. He was fluent in the Inuit language and he understood the Inuit culture. It was only because of Matt Henson that the Inuit agreed to make the treacherous four-hundred-mile trip to a

LOS ANGELES HERALD

40 CENTS _____ THURSDAY MORNING. SEPTEMBER 16. 1909.

NEGRO COMPANION OF PEARY TELLS OF TRIP

[By Associated Press.]

BATTLE HARBOR, Sept. 15.—"We hoisted the Stars and Stripes twice at the north pole," said Matthew Henson, Commander Robert E. Peary's negro lieutenant, and the only other civilized man, according to Peary, who ever reached the pole.

Hnesen then gave to the Associated Press an account of one night and two days he and Commander Peary and four Eskimos camped at 90 degrees north latitude.

Henson assisted in raising the American flag and he led the Eskimos in the cheer, an extra cheer for old glory in the Eskimo tongue being given.

"Having passed eighteen years with Commander Peary and a considerable portion of that time in the Arctic," said Henson, "I have acquired a knowledge of the dialect of northern Greenland Eskimos.

"We arrived at the pole just before noon April 6, the party consisting of the commander, myself, four Eskimos and thirty-six dogs, divided into two detachments in number and headed respectively by Commander Peary and myself.

Where They Left Party

"We had left the last supporting party at 87 degrees 53 minutes where we separated from Capt. Bartlett, who was photographed by the commander.

"Capt. Bartlett regretted that he did not have a British flag to erect on the ice at this spot, so that the photograph might show this as the farthest north to which the banner of Great Britain had been advanced.

"I kept a personal diary during this historic dash across the ice field. Our first task on reaching the pole was to build two igloos, as the weather was hazy and prevented taking accurate observation to confirm the distance traveled from Cape Columbia.

"Having completed the snow houses we had dinner, which included tea, and then retired to rest, thus sleeping one night at the north pole. The Arctic sun was shing when I awoke and found the commander already up. There was only wind enough to blow out the small flags.

"The ensigns were hoisted toward noon from the tent poles and tide with fish lines.

Didn't Go Beyond It

"We had figured out the distance pretty close and did not go beyond the pole.

"The flags were up about mid-day, April 7, and were not moved until late that evening. The haze had cleared away early, but we wanted some hours to make observations. We made three close together.

"When we first raised the American flag its position was behind the igloos, which, according to our initial observations, was the position of the pole, but on taking subsequent observations the stars and stripes were moved and placed 150 yards west of the first position, the difference in the observations being due, perhaps, to the moving ice.

"When the flag was placed Commander Peary exclaimed in English: 'We will plant the stars and stripes at the north pole.'

"In the native language I proposed three cheers, which were given in the Eskimos' own tongue. Commander Peary shook hands all around and we had a more liberal dinner than usual, each man eating as much as he pleased.

Eskimos Danced

"The Eskimos danced about and showed great pleasure that the pole at last was reached.

"For years the Eskimos had been trying to reach that spot, but it was always with them 'tiquelgh,' which translated means 'get so far and no closer.'

"We exclaimed in a chorus: 'Ting neigh timnah ketisher,' meaning 'We have got there at last.'"

Henson, who reached the farthest north with Peary three years ago, said that conditions were about the same at the pole as elsewhere in the Arctic circle. All was a solid sea of ice with a two-foot lead of open water two miles from the pole.

The Eskimos who went along on the final lap were Ootah, Egingwah, Ouzaueeah and Sigloo, the two first named being brothers. Commander Peary took photographs of Henson and the Eskimos waving flags and cheering.

"The report is absolutely untrue that I did not go to the pole," said Henson. "I went the whole distance."

Henson said he knew that some on board did not wish him to go to the pole if they could prevent it. He also said that he saw Peary write the records which were left in the ice.

Understood English

The Eskimos who were with them, with one exception, understood English.

"At the pole," continued Henson, "we could see no land and we went no distance beyond the flags. The ice near the igloos was at least ten feet high, and the flags were placed on a hummock twenty feet in height. The ice at the pole was about the same.

"Nearly all the winds we had were from the northeast. Commander Peary had three thermometers, and the coldest day was 57 degrees below zero Fahrenheit. I believe there is a little difference in the temperature at the north pole from that some distance south."

Henson learned from the Eskimos that for three days in Whale sound last month they saw a cloud of smoke and there was an odor like brimstone. The natives were greatly frightened, and Henson thought a new volcano had erupted, and so informed them.

Henson made his first trip north in 1891. He went there because he was interested, and kept on going year after year.

Of Commander Peary he said:

"He is the best man that we could have for Arctic expeditions. He has wonderful endurance and the weather never is too cold for him.

"Many times I would not leave the camp except for him. A compass course is all he desires. So long as a man does his work half decently, the commander never complains. The Eskimos think that there is no man like him."

Matthew Henson was born in Washington, but lived for a time in Florida. He is quite proud to be the only negro to go the farthest north. He is in good health, but lost twenty pounds in the sixty-eight days march to the pole and return.

The only frost bites he suffered were on the cheek and nose. He thinks some negroes can endure as much exposure as a white man, although he is not sure that he stood the cold the first year as well as his white companions.

Speaking of the Eskimos, Henson said they could draw as good a chart of that country as any person.

They do not know the length of a mile, but can estimate distance very exactly. To one who knows the language they will tell dates within a few days. They cannot take observations but they know what they are taken for.

Henson said that he would go to the south pole tomorrow if he had a chance, as he was interested in exploring and it would be hard to discontinue.

Newspapers and magazines wrote hundreds of accounts of the race to the North Pole.

place that looked absolutely no different to them from their starting point.[12] Without the Inuit, neither Henson nor Peary would have made it to the Pole.

Robert Peary chose Henson to accompany him because Henson was the man most suited for the job. But Peary probably had another reason as well. If he had taken Robert Bartlett to the Pole, he would have been forced to share with him the fame and coveted title "Discoverer of the North Pole." It was less likely that the same problem would exist with a black or Inuit at his side; indeed, there were few whites at that time who would consider a person of color as a possible co-discoverer of anything.

Robert Peary did little to change the attitudes of these prejudiced people. In his book about his experience at the Pole, he wrote that "if Henson had been sent back with one of the supporting parties . . . he would never have reached land. . . . he had not, as a racial inheritance, the daring and initiative of Bartlett."[13] Peary knew this to be untrue; in fact, without Henson leading him, Peary would not have made it back to Anniversary Lodge on the Second Greenland Expedition.

Without the utmost faith in Matt Henson's abilities, Peary would not have risked his life and future fame in a place so remote he could not be rescued. So why did Peary write something he did not believe? Did he think it was something that his readers would want to believe? This was a time in the United States when a partnership between a white man and a black man was uncommon—and to some it was unthinkable.

While Robert Peary was awarded many medals and promoted to the rank of admiral in the navy, Matt Henson received few honors. In October 1909, a group of prominent African-American leaders, including the Reverend Adam Clayton Powell, Sr., and Booker T. Washington, gave a dinner for Henson and presented him with a gold watch.[14] This evening must have been very special for Henson and his wife, Lucy. But there was little after that.

The only work that Matt Henson could find was as a parking lot attendant. He published a book in 1912 about his Arctic experiences entitled *A Negro Explorer at the North Pole*, but it did not sell many copies. Henson finally wrote to Peary about his trouble finding work, and Peary asked a friend in the government to help. Henson's friends also petitioned the president. Almost a year later, after President Taft signed an executive order that allowed Henson to be appointed to "any suitable position in the classified service," Henson became a clerk in the federal customs house in New York City.[15] He would stay at this same job until he retired nearly twenty-five years later.

From the time Henson returned from the Arctic until Robert Peary's death eleven years after, they saw each other only once. It seems almost incomprehensible

In 1912, Henson had this formal portrait taken to include in his book, *A Negro Explorer at the North Pole.*

that the relationship of two men who had lived so closely, whose very lives had been in the other's hands for more than eighteen years, could end so abruptly. But Peary adhered to the strict lines drawn by American society to divide the races—lines that had not been visible in the snow up north. In the Arctic, Henson's race was never the issue it was once he came back home.

Robert Peary died in 1920 and was buried in Arlington National Cemetery with a twenty-one-gun salute. President Warren G. Harding attended the funeral. Matt Henson read about the ceremonies in the newspaper. A friend reported that he cried.[16]

Almost thirty years after the Pole expedition, the renowned Explorers Club in New York City made Henson an honorary member. He was the first African American invited to join this select group of explorers from around the world. In 1946, the navy honored all the living members of the expedition, though there was no special mention of Henson's having reached the Pole. The next year, Bradley Robinson wrote a biography of Henson called *Dark Companion*. Newspapers and magazines did follow-up articles and reviews. Henson was interviewed on the radio and at eighty-two years of age received his first bit of fame.

In 1948, Donald MacMillan presented Henson with a gold medal from the Chicago Geographical Society. This recognition was the first from a geographic society

DARK
COMPANION

★
North Pole

MATTHEW HENSON
Conqueror of the Arctic Ice
Co-Discoverer of the Pole

BRADLEY ROBINSON

Introductions by   VILHJALMUR STEFANSSON

COMDR. DONALD B. MACMILLAN   PETER FREUCHEN

At eighty-two years of age, Matt Henson finally achieved some fame
after the publication of this biography by Bradley Robinson.

and was particularly meaningful to Henson.[17] In 1954, he and Lucy were invited to the White House to meet with President Dwight Eisenhower.

On March 9, 1955, Matthew Henson died at the age of eighty-eight. The Reverend Adam Clayton Powell, Jr., led his funeral service at the Abyssinian Baptist Church in Harlem in New York City. More than one thousand people attended the ceremony, after which Henson was buried in a very simple grave alongside his wife's mother.

Thirty-three years later, after an extraordinary effort on the part of Harvard professor S. Allen Counter, Matthew Henson was reburied in Arlington National Cemetery next to Robert Peary. His headstone reads "Matthew Alexander Henson, Co-Discoverer of the North Pole." The date of his reburial was April 6, 1988, the seventy-ninth anniversary of the expedition's great success.

Dr. Counter's research on Henson's life uncovered information that neither Henson nor Peary had made public during their lifetimes. Counter learned that each man had fathered a son with an Inuit woman. Dr. Counter traveled to the Arctic and reunited these men, both of whom were by this time in their eighties, with their relatives in the United States.

Matt Henson's son, Anaukaq, described to Counter the pride he had always felt at being the son of the beloved *Mahri-Pahluk* of the Inuit.[18] Anaukaq reported

Henson's bravery, survival skills, and bond with the Inuit people made Peary's quest for the North Pole a reality.

that since childhood he had learned many songs and stories about his father. To the Inuit people, Anaukaq said, Henson "was the most popular outsider ever to visit his land."[19]

In the decades after Robert Peary and Matthew Henson claimed the North Pole, much controversy surrounded them. Some people argued that Frederick Cook beat them to it. Others questioned whether an uneducated black man could be considered a credible eyewitness to a scientific milestone. Still others remained unconvinced that the team got there at all.

This last query was answered in one way by a study done in 1990 by the National Geographic Society. The society reported that although the men had used the most reliable navigational instruments available at the time—an artificial horizon and a sextant—the instruments may not have measured their position accurately. Peary and Henson may have ended their trek three to five miles short of their goal.[20]

There is another way to look at this debate. The North Pole is not a fixed point: It is under a perpetually moving ice cap. An exact position of the Pole can now be determined with sophisticated electronic equipment. Peary and Henson had only an artificial horizon and a sextant. Since they were without doubt very close to this continually shifting geographic area, it can be said assuredly that Robert Peary and Matt Henson were the first to reach the North Pole.

Peary and Henson were exceptionally adventurous, brave, and strong-willed. But they reached the top of the world because they had different talents and they combined forces. Robert Peary was the strategist: He raised the money and he planned the routes. Matthew Henson was the operations man: He kept things working. Theirs was a uniquely successful partnership.

Yet because he was an African American, Henson was never acknowledged in his lifetime as Peary's partner. In the foreword to Henson's book about the Pole, Peary wrote that Henson proved that "race, or color, or bringing-up, or environment, count nothing against a

This commemorative postage stamp was issued in 1986.

determined heart, if it is backed and aided by intelligence."[21] Unfortunately, Peary did nothing to convince others of this view and abandoned Henson himself once they returned to the United States.

Matt Henson was one of the most accomplished Arctic explorers in history. Being first at the North Pole should have made him a national hero. Instead, Henson was never adequately rewarded for his achievement. The second half of his life was not much easier than the first half.

In the Inuit culture, Matthew Henson has always been held in the highest esteem. He should be remembered with the same distinction by ours. After he became a commander in the U.S. Navy, Donald MacMillan was asked about Henson's contributions. With the straight talk of a military man, MacMillan said:

> From that day in early September when the *Roosevelt* stuck her stub nose into the ice-foot bordering the northern shore of Ellesmere Island, Henson, strong physically, and above all fully experienced, was of more real value to our Commander than Bartlett, Marvin, Borup, Goodsell and myself all put together. Matthew Henson went to the Pole with Peary because he was a better man than any of us.[22]

"A better man than any of us"—there are no better words to commemorate Matthew Henson.

CHRONOLOGY

1866—Matthew Alexander Henson is born August 8 in Charles County, Maryland.

1879—Begins five-year stint sailing with Captain Childs on the *Katie Hines*.

1887—Meets Robert Peary and goes with him to Nicaragua.

1891—First venture north to Greenland is successful; Henson marries Eva Flint.

1893—Second Greenland Expedition (ends in failure in 1895).

1896—Divorces Eva Flint; first of two trips to bring back meteorites from Cape York.

1897—Second trip to retrieve meteorites.

1898—Henson and Peary begin four continuous years in Arctic.

1902—Henson takes job as Pullman porter.

1905—Henson and Peary come within 200 miles of
–1906 the North Pole.

1907—Henson marries Lucy Ross.

1908—*Roosevelt* expedition leaves for second Pole attempt.

1909—North Pole discovered on April 6.

1912—Henson publishes a book about his experiences.

1913—Begins twenty-five-year job with Customs House in New York City.

1920—Robert Peary dies and is given a hero's burial in Arlington National Cemetery.

1937—Henson is invited to join the Explorers Club.

1946—Polar expedition is honored by navy.

1947—Bradley Robinson writes *Dark Companion*, Henson's biography.

1948—Henson receives a medal from the Chicago Geographical Society.

1954—Henson and his wife, Lucy, meet President Eisenhower.

1955—Henson dies March 9.

1986—The United States Postal Service issues a commemorative stamp in Henson's honor.

1988—Henson is reburied next to Peary in Arlington National Cemetery.

CHAPTER NOTES

Chapter 1. Close Call

1. Bradley Robinson and Matthew Henson, *Dark Companion, The Official Biography of Matthew Henson* (New York: Robert M. McBride & Company, 1948), p.146.

2. Ibid.

3. Ibid., p. 149.

4. John Edward Weems, *Peary, The Explorer and the Man* (Boston: Houghton Mifflin Company, 1967), p. 216.

5. Ibid.

6. Robinson and Henson, p.153.

7. Matthew Henson, *A Negro Explorer at the North Pole* (New York: Frederick A. Stokes Company, 1912), reprinted as *A Black Explorer at the North Pole* (University of Nebraska Press, 1989), p.13.

8. Robinson and Henson, p. 157.

Chapter 2. Seaworthy

1. James M. McPherson, *Battle Cry of Freedom: The Civil War Era* (New York: Ballantine Books, 1989), p. 284.

2. Bradley Robinson and Matthew Henson, *Dark Companion, The Official Biography of Matthew Henson* (New York: Robert M. McBride & Company, 1948), p.18.

3. Henson later said that his mother died in 1868 when he was two.

4. Robinson and Henson, pp. 19–21.

5. Ibid., p. 23.

6. Ibid., p. 26.

7. Ibid., p. 29.

8. Matthew Henson, *A Negro Explorer at the North Pole* (New York: Frederick A. Stokes Company, 1912), reprinted as *A Black Explorer at the North Pole* (Omaha: University of Nebraska Press, 1989), p. 3.

9. Ibid.

10. Robinson and Henson, p. 43.

11. Ibid.

12. Ibid., p. 50.

13. Ibid.

14. Henson, p. 3.

Chapter 3. Blueprint for a Canal

1. John Edward Weems, *Peary, The Explorer and the Man* (Boston: Houghton Mifflin Company, 1967), p. 85.

2. Ibid., p. 90.

3. Bradley Robinson and Matthew Henson, *Dark Companion, The Official Biography of Matthew Henson* (New York: Robert M. McBride & Company, 1948), p. 52.

4. Robert E. Peary, *Northward Over the Great Ice* (New York: Frederick A. Stokes Company, 1898), vol. 1, p. 47.

5. Letter dated August 16, 1880, from Robert Peary to his mother, reprinted in Weems, p. 3.

6. Peary, *Northward*, vol. 1, pp. xxxiii-iv.

7. Letter from Robert Peary to his mother dated February 27, 1887, reprinted in Robert M. Bryce, *Cook & Peary, The Polar Controversy Resolved* (Mechanicsburg, Pa.: Stackpole Books, 1997) p. 22.

8. Marie Peary Stafford, *Discoverer of the North Pole*, p. 78, reprinted in Weems, p. 99.

9. Matthew Henson, *A Negro Explorer at the North Pole* (New York, Frederick A. Stokes Company, 1912), reprinted as *A Black Explorer at the North Pole* (Omaha: University of Nebraska Press, 1989), p. 3.

10. S. Allen Counter, *North Pole Legacy: Black, White and Eskimo* (Amherst: University of Massachusetts Press, 1991), p. 56.

11. Robinson and Henson, p. 54.

12. Letter from John Verhoeff to Robert Peary dated March 16, 1891, reprinted in Bryce, p. 26.

13. Bryce, p. 33.

14. Ibid., p. 27.

15. Henson, p. 6.

Chapter 4. Trailblazers

1. Bradley Robinson and Matthew Henson, *Dark Companion, The Official Biography of Matthew Henson* (New York: Robert M. McBride & Company, 1948), p. 55.

2. *The New York Times*, June 7, 1891, reprinted in Robert M. Bryce, *Cook & Peary: The Polar Controversy Resolved* (Mechanicsburg, Pa.: Stackpole Books, 1997), p. 27.

3. Ibid., p. 28.

4. John Edward Weems, *Peary, The Explorer and the Man* (Boston: Houghton Mifflin Company, 1967), p.109.

5. Barry Lopez, *Arctic Dreams* (New York: Bantam Books, 1996), p. 208.

6. Robinson and Henson, p. 57.

7. Weems, p. 111.

8. Ibid., p. 113.

9. Bryce, p. 39.

10. Robinson and Henson, p. 57.

11. Bryce, p. 40.

12. Matthew Henson, *A Negro Explorer at the North Pole* (New York: Frederick A. Stokes Company, 1912), reprinted as *A Black Explorer at the North Pole* (Omaha University of Nebraska Press, 1989), p. 29.

13. S. Allen Counter, *North Pole Legacy: Black, White and Eskimo* (Amherst: University of Massachusetts Press, 1991), p. 7.

14. Ibid., pp. 215, 217–218.

15. Henson, pp. 6–7.

16. Counter, p. 4.

17. Peter Freuchen, *"Ahdolo, Ahdolo!"* March 18, 1947, article reprinted in Counter, p. 70.

18. Counter, p. 7.

19. Robinson and Henson, p. 58.

20. Bryce, p. 45.

21. Robinson and Henson, p. 65.

22. Ibid., p. 59.

23. Ibid.

24. Robert E. Peary, *The North Pole, Its Discovery in 1909 Under the Auspices of the Peary Arctic Club* (New York: Frederick A. Stokes Company, 1910), p. 20.

25. Barry Lopez, *Arctic Dreams* (New York: Bantam Books, 1996), p. 243.

26. Bryce, p. 66.

27. Counter, p. 124.

28. Henson, p. 6.

Chapter 5. "The Long Race with Death"

1. Robert M. Bryce, *Cook & Peary, The Polar Controversy Resolved* (Mechanicsburg, Pennsylvania: Stackpole Books, 1997), p. 87.

2. Ibid.

3. John Edward Weems, *Peary, The Explorer and the Man* (Boston: Houghton Mifflin Company, 1967), p. 128.

4. Ibid., pp. 129–130.

5. Bradley Robinson and Matthew Henson, *Dark Companion, The Official Biography of Matthew Henson* (New York: Robert M. McBride & Company, 1948), p. 70.

6. Weems, p. 131.

7. Ibid., p. 137.

8. Robinson and Henson, p. 71.

9. Robert E. Peary, *Northward Over the Great Ice* (New York: Frederick A. Stokes Company, 1898), vol. 2, pp. 97–100.

10. Weems, p. 143.

11. Ibid., p. 145.

12. Matthew Henson, *A Negro Explorer at the North Pole* (New York: Frederick A. Stokes Company, 1912), reprinted as *A Black Explorer at the North Pole* (Omaha: University of Nebraska Press, 1989), p. 3.

13. Letter from Robert E. Peary to his wife dated March 31, 1895, reprinted in Weems, p. 155.

14. Weems, p. 157.

15. Henson, p. 9.

16. Robinson and Henson, p. 89.

17. Ibid., pp. 92–95.

18. Ibid., p. 101.

19. Weems, p. 142.

Chapter 6. Marathon

1. Robert M. Bryce, *Cook & Peary, The Polar Controversy Resolved* (Mechanicsburg, Pa.: Stackpole Books, 1997), p. 207.

2. Bradley Robinson and Matthew Henson, *Dark Companion, The Official Biography of Matthew Henson* (New York: Robert M. McBride & Company, 1948), p. 99.

3. S. Allen Counter, *North Pole Legacy: Black, White and Eskimo* (Amherst: University of Massachusetts Press, 1991), p. 60.

4. Robinson and Henson, p. 100.

5. Robert E. Peary, *The North Pole, Its Discovery in 1909 Under the Auspices of the Peary Arctic Club* (New York: Frederick A. Stokes Company, 1910), p. 13.

6. Bryce, p. 209.

7. Barry Lopez, *Arctic Dreams* (New York: Bantam Books, 1996), p. 281.

8. Robert Peary's diary dated January 6, 1899, reprinted in John Edward Weems, *Peary, the Explorer and the Man* (Boston: Houghton Mifflin Company, 1967), pp. 179–180.

9. Lopez, p. 365.

10. Robinson and Henson, p. 129.

11. Ibid., pp. 131–132.

12. Bryce, p. 228.

13. Weems, p. 198.

14. Robinson and Henson, p. 133.

15. Matthew Henson, *A Negro Explorer At the North Pole* (New York: Frederick A. Stokes Company, 1912), reprinted as *A Black Explorer at the North Pole* (Omaha: University of Nebraska Press, 1989), p. 84.

16. Ibid., p. 11.

17. Weems, p. 199.

18. Henson, p. 12.

Chapter 7. Farthest North

1. Barry Lopez, *Arctic Dreams* (New York: Bantam Books, 1996), pp. 372–373.

2. John Edward Weems, *Peary, The Explorer and the Man* (Boston: Houghton Mifflin Company, 1967), p. 176.

3. Robert M. Bryce, *Cook & Peary, The Polar Controversy Resolved* (Mechanicsburg, Pennsylvania: Stackpole Books, 1997), p. 265.

4. Weems, p. 202.

5. Bradley Robinson and Matthew Henson, *Dark Companion, The Official Biography of Matthew Henson* (New York: Robert M. McBride & Company, 1948), p. 136.

6. Ibid., pp. 137–138.

7. Ibid.

8. Ibid., p. 139.

9. Ibid., p. 145.

10. Arthur M. Schlesinger, Jr., and Fred Israel, eds., *Robert E. Peary and the Rush to the North Pole, Chronicles from National Geographic* (Philadelphia: Chelsea House, 1999), p. 21.

11. Ibid., p. 10.

12. Bryce, p. 265.

13. Robinson and Henson, p. 146.

14. Matthew Henson, *A Negro Explorer at the North Pole* (New York: Frederick A. Stokes Company, 1912), reprinted as *A Black Explorer at the North Pole* (Omaha: University of Nebraska Press), p. 13.

15. Robinson and Henson, p. 148.

16. Weems, pp. 211–212.

17. Ibid., p. 214.

18. Robinson and Henson, p. 149.

19. Weems, p. 216.

20. Robert E. Peary, *Nearest the Pole*, pp. 144–146, reprinted in Weems, pp. 219–220.

21. Ibid., p. 222.

22. Robinson and Henson, p. 157.

23. Weems, p. 225.

Chapter 8. "The Prize of Three Centuries"

1. Robert E. Peary, *The North Pole, Its Discovery In 1909 Under the Auspices of the Peary Arctic Club* (New York: Frederick A. Stokes Company, 1910), pp. 17–18.

2. Ibid., pp. 4–5.

3. Ibid., pp. 16–17.

4. Bradley Robinson and Matthew Henson, *Dark Companion, The Official Biography of Matthew Henson* (New York: Robert M. McBride & Company, 1948), p. 164.

5. Ibid., p. 159.

6. Matthew Henson, *A Negro Explorer At the North Pole* (New York: Frederick A. Stokes Company, 1912), reprinted as *A Black Explorer at the North Pole* (Omaha: University of Nebraska Press, 1989), pp. 40–41.

7. Peary, p. 24.

8. Ibid., p. 31.

9. Ibid., p. 25.

10. Ibid., p. 27.

11. Henson, p. 16.

12. Ibid., p. 26.

13. John Edward Weems, Peary, *The Explorer and the Man* (Boston: Houghton Mifflin Company, 1967), p. 239.

14. Terry Jennings, *Polar Regions* (Danbury, Conn.: Grolier Educational Corp., 1992), vol. 4, p. 5.

15. Peary, p. 115.

16. Ibid., pp. 129–130.

17. Henson, pp. 112–113.

18. Weems, p. 241.

19. Robinson and Henson, p. 168.

20. Henson, p. 95.

21. Peary, p. 228.

22. Robinson and Henson, p. 170.

23. Henson, p. 113.

24. Peary, p. 265.

25. Henson, pp. 129–130.

26. Ibid., pp. 130–131.

27. *New York Times*, "First Report By Commander Robert E. Peary, U.S.N., September 6, 1909," reprinted in Arthur M. Schlesinger, Jr., and Fred Israel, eds., *Robert E. Peary and the Rush to the North Pole, Chronicles From National Geographic* (Philadelphia: Chelsea House, 1999), p.78.

28. Robinson, p. 174.

29. Peary, p. 287.

30. Henson, p. 136.

31. Ibid.

32. Ibid., p. 143.

33. Robinson and Henson, p. 181.

Chapter 9. After the Arctic

1. Bradley Robinson and Matthew Henson, *Dark Companion, The Official Biography of Matthew Henson* (New York: Robert McBride & Company, 1948), pp. 180–181.

2. Robert M. Bryce, *Cook & Peary, The Polar Controversy Resolved* (Mechanicsburg, Pa.: Stackpole Books, 1997), p. 369.

3. Robert E. Peary, *The North Pole, Its Discovery In 1909 Under the Auspices of the Peary Arctic Club* (New York: Frederick A. Stokes Company, 1910), p. 318.

4. S. Allen Counter, *North Pole Legacy: Black, White, and Eskimo* (Amherst: University of Massachusetts Press, 1991), p. 66.

5. *New York World*, September 22, 1909, as reprinted in Bryce, p. 394.

6. *New York Herald*, September 8, 1909, as reprinted in Bryce, p. 366.

7. John Edward Weems, *Peary, The Explorer and the Man* (Boston: Houghton Mifflin Company, 1967), p. 281.

8. "The North Pole," in *National Geographic* (November 1909), as reprinted in Arthur M. Schlesinger, Jr., and Fred Israel, eds., *Robert E. Peary and the Rush to the North Pole* (Philadelphia: Chelsea House, 1999), p. 87.

9. Counter, pp. 200–201.

10. Donald B. MacMillan, "Peary as a Leader: Incidents from the Life of the Discoverer of the North Pole Told by One of His Lieutenants on the Expedition Which Reached the Goal," in *National Geographic* (April 1920), as reprinted in Schlesinger and Israel, p. 116.

11. Peary, p. 272.

12. Robinson and Henson, p. 176.

13. Peary, p. 273.

14. Counter, p. 72.

15. Ibid., p. 74.

16. Ibid.

17. Ibid., p. 75.

18. Ibid., p. 7.

19. Ibid.

20. Thomas D. Davies, Rear Admiral U.S.N. (Ret.), "New Evidence Places Peary at the Pole," *National Geographic* (January 1990), p. 46.

21. Matthew Henson, *A Negro Explorer at the North Pole* (New York: Frederick A. Stokes Company, 1912), reprinted as *A Black Explorer at the North Pole* (Omaha: University of Nebraska Press, 1989), p. xxvii.

22. MacMillan, as reprinted in Verne Robinson, "Did Henson & Peary Reach the North Pole?", 1997, <http://www.matthewhenson.com/didthey.html> (July 16, 2000).

FURTHER READING

Counter, S. Allen. *North Pole Legacy: Black, White and Eskimo.* Amherst: University of Massachusetts Press, 1991.

Ferris, Jeri. *Arctic Explorer: The Story of Matthew Henson,* Minneapolis: Carolrhoda Books, Inc., 1989.

Gilman, Michael. *Matthew Henson, Explorer.* New York: Chelsea House Publishers, 1988.

Henson, Matthew. *A Negro Explorer at the North Pole.* New York: Frederick A. Stokes Co., 1912. Reprinted as *A Black Explorer at the North Pole.* Omaha: University of Nebraska Press, 1989.

Peary, Robert E. *The North Pole: Its Discovery in 1909 Under the Auspices of the Peary Arctic Club.* New York: Frederick A. Stokes Co., 1910.

Robinson, Bradley, *Dark Companion: The Story of Matthew Henson.* New York: Robert M. McBride & Co., 1948.

Schlesinger, Arthur M., Jr., and Israel, Fred, eds., *Robert E. Peary and the Rush to the North Pole.* Philadelphia: Chelsea House Publishers, 1999.

Williams, Jean Kinney. *Matthew Henson: Polar Adventurer.* New York: Franklin Watts, 1994.

INTERNET ADDRESSES

<http://www.matthewhenson.com>
This is the most comprehensive site on the web and has links to other information.

<http://www.northpole-expeditions.com/vj/vj1.html>

<http://www.childlight.com/northpole/html_pages/ northpole_home.htm>

INDEX

Page numbers for photographs are in **boldface** type.